W9-CQY-352

CROCK·POT®
SLOW COOKER
CUISINE

RIVAL®

Cover photography by Kathy Ketner.

Food Styling by Marta Bainum.

Copyright © 1995 by Rival Manufacturing Company.
All rights reserved. No portion of this book may be reprinted
or reproduced in any form or any manner without the written
permission of the publishers, except by a reviewer who wishes
to quote brief passages in connection with a review.

Produced in the United States of America.

Library of Congress Catalog Card Number: 75-15197

Crock-Pot® is a trademark of Rival Manufacturing Company,
Kansas City, Missouri. Registration Number: 928,614.

Golden and Golden Press are trademarks of
Western Publishing Company, Inc.

This book is dedicated to the Crock-Pot® Cook —

With today's busy schedules, the Crock-Pot slow cooker has become an integral appliance in the kitchen. As most of you already know, you simply place the ingredients in the Crock-Pot, plug it in and turn it on. This leaves you free to spend the day as you like, all the while assured that when you return a delicious meal will be ready and waiting. No more last minute panic of what to fix for dinner.

Taking into consideration our hectic lives and the need or desire for healthier eating, we have pooled together a collection of tantalizing recipes which we feel are in tune with today's lifestyles. Just look for this symbol: , for the recipes that are quick and easy.

This cookbook is filled with over 100 new recipes as well as over 100 tried and true recipe favorites. So what are you waiting for? Plug in that Crock-Pot and get cooking!

The Home Economics Department
The Rival Company

CONTENTS

APPETIZERS AND BEVERAGES

CHICKEN WINGS IN BBQ SAUCE

3	pounds chicken wings (16 wings)
	salt and pepper to taste
1½	cups any variety barbecue sauce
¼	cup honey
2	teaspoons prepared mustard or spicy mustard
2	teaspoons Worcestershire sauce
	Tabasco to taste, optional

Rinse chicken and pat dry. Cut off and discard wing tips. Cut each wing at joint to make two sections. Sprinkle wing parts with salt and pepper. Place wings on a broiler pan. Broil 4 to 5 inches from the heat for 20 minutes, 10 minutes for each side or until chicken is brown. Transfer chicken to Crock-Pot.

For sauce, combine barbecue sauce, honey, mustard, Worcestershire sauce, and if more heat is desired Tabasco to taste in a small mixing bowl. Pour over chicken wings. Cover and cook on Low for 4 to 5 hours or on High 2 to 2½ hours. Serve directly from Crock-Pot. *Makes about 32 appetizers.*

CHICKEN WINGS IN TERIYAKI SAUCE

3	pounds chicken wings (16 wings)
1	large onion, chopped
1	cup soy sauce
1	cup brown sugar
2	teaspoons ground ginger

2   **cloves garlic, minced**
¼   **cup dry cooking sherry**

Rinse chicken and pat dry. Cut off and discard wing tips. Cut each wing at joint to make two sections. Place wing parts on broiler pan. Broil 4 to 5 inches from the heat for 20 minutes, 10 minutes for each side or until chicken is brown. Transfer chicken to Crock-Pot.

Mix together onion, soy sauce, brown sugar, ginger, garlic, and cooking sherry in bowl. Pour over chicken wings. Cover and cook on Low 5 to 6 hours or on High 2 to 3 hours. Stir chicken wings once to ensure wings are evenly coated with sauce. Serve from Crock-Pot. *Makes about 32 appetizers.*

SPICY FRANKS

This fast and easy to prepare appetizer can usually be made from ingredients on hand.

1   **cup catsup**
¼   **cup firmly packed light brown sugar**
1   **tablespoon red wine vinegar**
2   **teaspoons soy sauce**
2   **teaspoons Dijon–style mustard**
⅛   **teaspoon garlic powder**
1   **pound frankfurters, cut in 1–inch pieces, or 1 pound cocktail weiners, or smoked sausages**

Place catsup, brown sugar, vinegar, soy sauce, mustard, and garlic in Crock-Pot. Cover and cook on High until blended, 1 to 2 hours. Stir in frankfurters. Cook until thoroughly heated, 1 to 2 hours. Turn to Low to keep warm and serve from Crock-Pot.

CHICKEN WINGS IN HONEY SAUCE

3   pounds chicken wings (16 wings)
    salt and pepper to taste
2   cups honey
½   cup ketchup
1   cup soy sauce
¼   cup oil
2   cloves garlic, minced
    sesame seeds, optional for garnish

Rinse chicken and pat dry. Cut off and discard wing tips. Cut each wing at joint to make two sections. Sprinkle wing parts with salt and pepper. Place wings on a broiler pan. Broil 4 to 5 inches from the heat for 20 minutes, 10 minutes for each side or until chicken is brown. Transfer chicken to Crock-Pot.

For sauce, combine honey, ketchup, soy sauce, oil, and garlic in mixing bowl. Pour over chicken wings. Cover and cook on Low 4 to 5 hours or on High 2 to 2½ hours. If desired garnish with sesame seeds. *Makes about 32 appetizers.*

MARINERS' FONDUE

2   cans (10¾ ounces each) condensed cream of celery soup
2   cups grated sharp process cheese
1   cup chunked cooked lobster
½   cup chopped cooked shrimp
½   cup chopped cooked crabmeat

1/4   cup finely chopped, cooked scallops
     dash paprika
     dash cayenne pepper
1   loaf French bread, cut into 1-inch cubes

Combine all ingredients except bread cubes in lightly greased Crock-Pot; stir thoroughly. Cover and cook on High for 1 hour or until cheese is melted. Turn to Low for serving. Using fondue forks, dip bread cubes into fondue. *About 1 1/2 quarts.*

HOT REFRIED BEAN DIP

1   can (16 ounces) refried beans, drained and mashed
1/4   pound lean ground beef
3   tablespoons bacon fat
1   pound process American cheese, cubed
1-3   tablespoons taco sauce
1   tablespoon taco spice
     garlic salt

In skillet, brown beans and ground beef well in bacon fat. Add to Crock-Pot. Stir in remaining ingredients. Cover and cook on High until cheese is melted, about 1 to 2 hours, stirring occasionally. Turn to Low until ready to serve, up to 6 hours. Serve with warm tortilla chips. *About 1 1/2 quarts.*

BBQ MEATBALLS

Meatballs:
- 2 pounds ground beef
- 1 cup onion flavored bread crumbs or plain–flavored crumbs
- 1 teaspoon garlic powder
- 2 packages onion soup mix
- 2 teaspoons Worcestershire sauce
- 2 eggs

In large bowl combine all ingredients. Shape into meatballs. Brown in skillet with 1 tablespoon oil. Drain on paper towel. *Makes about 60 meatballs.*

BBQ Sauce:
- 2 large onions, chopped
- 2 (6 ounces each) cans tomato paste
- 2 cloves garlic, minced
- 1/4 cup Worcestershire sauce
- 1/4 cup red wine vinegar
- 1/2 cup brown sugar
- 1/2 cup sweet pickle relish
- 1/2 cup beef broth
- 2 teaspoons salt
- 2 teaspoons dry mustard

Add sauce ingredients to Crock-Pot and stir well. Place meatballs in Crock-Pot and cook on Low for 5 to 6 hours or on High for 2 to 3 hours or until hot. Serve directly from Crock-Pot.

"HOT" CHEESE AND BACON DIP

16 slices bacon, diced
2 packages (8 ounces each) cream cheese, softened, cut in cubes
4 cups mild shredded cheddar cheese
1 cup half–and–half
2 teaspoons Worcestershire sauce
1 teaspoon dry minced onion
$1/2$ teaspoon dry mustard
$1/2$ teaspoon salt
2-3 drops Tabasco sauce

Fry diced bacon in a skillet until crisp; drain on paper towels and set aside. Place cream cheese, cheddar cheese, half-and-half, Worcestershire sauce, minced onion, mustard, salt, and Tabasco in the Crock-Pot. Set on Low and allow cheese to melt, stirring occasionally for about 1 hour. Taste and adjust seasonings. Then stir in bacon and serve directly from Crock-Pot. Serve with fruit slices such as apples or pears or serve with French bread slices.

TIP: *If serving with fruit slices, dip fruit slices in lemon juice to prevent browning.*

HAMBURGER DIP

2   pounds lean ground beef

1   cup chopped onion

2   cloves garlic, minced (or $1/4$ teaspoon garlic powder)

     salt to taste

2   cans (8 ounces each) tomato sauce

$1/2$ cup ketchup

$1 1/2$ teaspoons oregano

2   teaspoons white granulated sugar

2   packages (8 ounces each) cream cheese, softened, cut in cubes

$2/3$ cup grated Parmesan cheese

1   teaspoon mild chili powder

In skillet brown ground beef with onion, discard fat. Pour browned meat and onion into Crock-Pot. Add garlic, salt, tomato sauce, ketchup, oregano, sugar, cream cheese, Parmesan cheese, and chili powder. Set Crock-Pot on Low until cream cheese has melted and is thoroughly blended, $1 1/2$ to 2 hours. Stir, taste and adjust seasoning if desired. Serve with cube French bread or tortilla chips.

If spicier dip is desired, use "hot" chili powder in place of mild chili powder.

HOT BROCCOLI-CHEESE DIP

3/4 cup butter

3 stalks celery, thinly sliced

1 medium onion, chopped

1 can (4 ounces) sliced mushrooms, drained

3 tablespoons flour

1 can (10½ ounces) condensed cream of celery soup

1 garlic cheese roll (5 to 6 ounces), cut up

1 package (10 ounces) frozen broccoli spears or chopped broccoli, thawed

In small skillet, melt butter and sauté celery, onion and mushrooms. Stir in flour. Turn into lightly greased Crock-Pot; stir in remaining ingredients. Cover and cook on High, stirring about every 15 minutes, until cheese is melted. Turn to Low for about 2 to 4 hours or until ready to serve. Serve hot with corn chips, raw cauliflowerets, carrot strips, celery chunks and radishes. *About 1 quart.*

PARTY MIX

2   cups O-shaped oat cereal
3   cups bite-size rice cereal
2   cups bite-size shredded wheat cereal
1   cup peanuts, pecans or cashews
1   cup thin pretzel sticks (optional)
½   cup butter or margarine, melted
4   tablespoons Worcestershire sauce
     dash Tabasco sauce
½   teaspoon seasoned salt
½   teaspoon garlic salt
½   teaspoon onion salt

Combine cereals, nuts and pretzels in Crock-Pot. Mix melted butter with all remaining ingredients; pour over cereal mixture in Crock-Pot and toss lightly to coat. Do not cover Crock-Pot. Cook on High for 2 hours, stirring well every 30 minutes; then turn to Low for 2 to 6 hours. Store in airtight container. *Makes 10 cups.*

HOT CRANBERRY TEA

This drink is perfect for an afternoon tea or for simply relaxing by the fire

1   package (8 ounces) fresh cranberries
3   quarts water
2   cups sugar
1   cup cinnamon red hots
24   whole cloves

3 cinnamon sticks
3 oranges
3 lemons

Boil cranberries in 1 quart of water for 10 minutes; set aside. Mix in 4, 5 or 6 quart Crock-Pot, 2 quarts water, sugar, red hots, cloves, cinnamon sticks; cover and heat on high until red hots dissolve, approximately 1 hour. Strain cranberry mixture and stir into Crock-Pot. Mix in the juice from oranges and lemons. Cover and heat 2 hours on High, turn to Low to keep warm and serve directly from the Crock-Pot.

SPICY PEACH PUNCH

For a change during the holidays, try this hot spiced punch.

1 jar (46 ounces) peach nectar
1 jar (20 ounces) orange juice
2 tablespoons + $1/2$ cup light brown sugar
1 cinnamon stick
$3/4$ teaspoon whole cloves
1 tablespoon lime juice

Combine peach nectar, orange juice, and brown sugar in Crock-Pot. Tie spice in cheesecloth bag or add loosely to punch. Cover and set on Low for 2 hours or on High for 1 hour. Stir in sugar and lime juice. Allow sugar to dissolve, approximately 30 minutes. Adjust to taste. Turn to Low to keep punch warm. Serve from Crock-Pot.

WARM FRUIT PUNCH

Warm up with a spiced punch laced with citrus — a nice alternative to spiced cider.

- 8 cups water
- 1 can (12 ounces) frozen cranberry–raspberry juice concentrate, thawed
- 1 can (12 ounces) frozen orange juice concentrate, thawed
- 1 can (6 ounces) frozen lemonade concentrate, thawed
- 1/2 cup sugar
- 4 cinnamon sticks
- 1/4 teaspoon whole cloves
- 1/4 teaspoon whole allspice
  - garnish: thin orange slice halves, unpeeled

In a 6-quart Crock-Pot, combine all ingredients. The spices can be tied in a cheesecloth and placed in punch if desired. Cover and heat on High for 3 hours, then turn to Low. Remove spices from Crock-Pot with a small strainer or slotted spoon. Serve directly from Crock-Pot. Garnish with orange slice halves if desired.

ORANGE-CIDER PUNCH

- 1 cup sugar
- 2 cinnamon sticks
- 1 whole nutmeg
- 2 cups apple cider or apple juice

6 cups orange juice
2 cups vodka (optional)

Mix all ingredients except vodka in Crock-Pot; stir well. Cover and cook on Low for 4 to 10 hours (on High for 2 to 3 hours). Just before serving, stir in vodka. Serve hot, in punch cups. *Serves 10 to 15 (about 2¹/₂ quarts).*

HOT CRANBERRY PUNCH

4 cups unsweetened pineapple juice
4 cups cranberry juice
¹/₂ cup brown sugar (packed)
1 cup water
1 teaspoon whole cloves and 1 cinnamon stick tied in cheesecloth
1-2 cups vodka

Combine all ingredients except vodka in Crock-Pot. Cover and cook on Low for 4 to 10 hours. Add vodka before serving. Serve hot, in punch cups. *Serves 10 to 15 (about 2¹/₂ quarts).*

HOT SPICED WINE

- 2 bottles dry red wine
- 3 apples, peeled, cored and thinly sliced
- 3 whole cloves
- 2 cinnamon sticks
- ½ cup sugar
- 1 teaspoon lemon juice

Combine all ingredients in Crock-Pot; stir well. Cover and cook on Low for 4 to 12 hours (on High for 1 to 2 hours). Serve hot, in punch cups or mugs. *Serves 6 to 8 (about 2 quarts).*

HOT SPICED CHERRY CIDER

- 3½ quarts apple cider
- 2 cinnamon sticks
- 2 packages (3 ounces each) cherry–flavored gelatin

In a 4, 5, or 6 quart Crock-Pot, mix together the apple cider and cinnamon sticks. Heat on High 3 hours. Stir in cherry–flavored gelatin. Keep on High 1 more hour and allow gelatin to dissolve. Turn to Low to keep warm. Serve directly from Crock-Pot.

BEEF, PORK AND LAMB

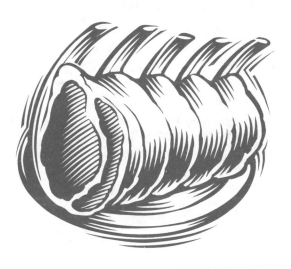

BARBECUED BEEF

This fast and easy BBQ beef recipe uses a tangy BBQ sauce, however for an even faster recipe use a bottled BBQ sauce.

3	pounds boneless chuck roast
1½	cups ketchup
2	tablespoons Dijon-style mustard
¼	cup packed brown sugar
¼	cup red wine vinegar
2	tablespoons Worcestershire sauce
1	teaspoon liquid smoke flavoring
½	teaspoon salt
¼	teaspoon pepper
¼	teaspoon garlic powder

Place chuck roast in Crock-Pot. Combine remaining ingredients in mixing bowl. Pour barbecue sauce mixture over chuck roast. Cover and cook on Low 8 to 10 hours or 4 to 5 hours on High. Remove chuck roast from Crock-Pot and shred meat. Place shredded meat back in Crock-Pot. Stir meat to evenly coat with sauce. Spoon meat onto sandwich buns and top with additional barbecue sauce if desired *Serves 12.*

Each Serving:	Calories 348 kcal	Protein 20 gm
	Fat 23 gm	Carbohydrate 13 gm
	Sodium 617 mg	Cholesterol 82 mg

POT ROAST
OVER NOODLES

2-2½ pounds beef chuck roast
1   tablespoon cooking oil
2   medium carrots, chopped
2   stalks celery, sliced
1   medium onion, sliced
2   cloves garlic minced
1   tablespoon quick-cooking tapioca
1   can (14½ ounces) Italian-style stewed tomatoes
1   can (6 ounces) Italian-style tomato paste
1   tablespoon brown sugar
½   teaspoon salt
½   teaspoon black pepper
1   bay leaf
1   package (8 ounces) hot cooked wide noodles

In a large skillet brown roast on all sides in hot oil. Transfer to any size Crock-Pot.

In a small bowl combine tomatoes, tomato paste, brown sugar, salt, pepper, and bay leaf; pour over meat. Cover and cook on Low for 10 to 12 hours or on High for 5 to 6 hours. Discard bay leaf. Cut meat up and serve over hot cooked noodles. *Serves 8.*

Each Serving:	Calories 513 kcal	Protein 28 gm
	Fat 29 gm	Carbohydrate 35 gm
	Sodium 598 mg	Cholesterol 119 mg

BEEF FAJITAS

1½	pounds beef flank steak
1	cup chopped onion
1	green sweet pepper, cut into ½-inch pieces
1	jalapeño pepper, chopped
1	tablespoon cilantro
2	cloves garlic, minced or ¼ teaspoon garlic powder
1	teaspoon chili powder
1	teaspoon ground cumin
1	teaspoon ground coriander
½	teaspoon salt
1	can (8 ounces) chopped tomatoes
12	8-inch flour tortillas

Toppings: sour cream, guacamole, shredded cheddar cheese, salsa

Cut flank steak into 6 portions. In any size Crock-Pot combine meat, onion, green sweet pepper, jalapeño pepper, cilantro, garlic, chili powder, cumin, coriander, and salt. Add tomatoes. Cover and cook on Low for 8 to 10 hours or on High 4 to 5 hours.

Remove meat from Crock-Pot and shred. Return meat to Crock-Pot and stir. To serve fajitas, spread meat mixture into flour tortillas and top with above mentioned toppings if desired. Roll up tortillas. *Serves 12.*

Tip: If using fresh jalapeños, be very careful in handling. Wear rubber gloves if possible as chili peppers contain a volatile oil that will burn if left in direct contact with the skin. Wash hands immediately after handling.

Each Serving:	Calories 229 kcal	Protein 15 gm
	Fat 9 gm	Carbohydrate 22 gm
	Sodium 287 mg	Cholesterol 30 mg

SLOPPY JOES

3	pounds ground beef
1	cup chopped onion
2	cloves garlic, minced or $1/4$ teaspoon garlic powder
$1^{1}/2$	cups ketchup
1	cup chopped green sweet pepper
$1/2$	cup water
4	tablespoons brown sugar
4	tablespoons prepared mustard
4	tablespoons vinegar
4	tablespoons Worcestershire sauce
3	teaspoons chili powder
	hamburger buns

In a large skillet brown ground beef, onion, and garlic. Cook until meat is brown and onion is tender. Drain off fat.

In any size Crock-Pot, combine ketchup, green sweet pepper, water, brown sugar, mustard, vinegar, Worcestershire sauce, and chili powder. Stir in meat mixture. Cover and cook on Low 6 to 8 hours or High 3 to 4 hours. Spoon into hamburger buns. *Serves 8 to 10.*

Variation: Substitute ground turkey, chicken, or pork in place of the ground beef.

Each Serving:	Calories 573 kcal	Protein 30 gm
	Fat 30 gm	Carbohydrate 43 gm
	Sodium 983 mg	Cholesterol 101 mg

MEAT LOAF ITALIAN-STYLE

This Italian-Style Meat Loaf can be formed the night before, refrigerated and then cooked in the Crock-Pot the next day.

1	can (8 ounces) pizza sauce
1	beaten egg
1/2	cup chopped onion
1/2	cup chopped green sweet pepper
1/3	cup dry seasoned bread crumbs
1/2	teaspoon garlic salt
1/4	teaspoon black pepper
1 1/2	pounds ground beef
1	cup shredded mozzarella cheese

Reserve 1/3 cup pizza sauce; cover and refrigerate. In a mixing bowl combine remaining pizza sauce and egg. Stir in onion, green pepper, bread crumbs, garlic salt, and black pepper. Add ground beef and mix well.

Fold meat mixture into a loaf and place on 3 strips of foil as described on Page 219. Transfer loaf to any size Crock-Pot. Cover and cook 8 to 10 hours on Low or 4 to 6 hours on High. To ensure doneness insert meat thermometer into center of loaf and internal temperature should read 170°.

Spread loaf with reserve 1/3 cup pizza sauce. Sprinkle with mozzarella cheese. Cover and let cook 15 minutes more or until cheese is melted. Using foil strips, lift loaf from Crock-Pot and transfer to a serving plate. Discard foil strips. Serve. *Serves 8.*

Each Serving:	Calories 260 kcal	Protein 19 gm
	Fat 17 gm	Carbohydrate 7 gm
	Sodium 436 mg	Cholesterol 90 mg

TOSTADA PIE

2 teaspoons cooking oil or olive oil
2 pounds ground beef
2 teaspoons chili powder
1 teaspoon ground cumin
1½ cups chopped onion
1 teaspoon salt
2 cloves garlic, minced or
   ¼ teaspoon garlic powder
1 can (16 ounces) tomato sauce
1 cup sliced black olives
8 corn tortillas
   soft margarine or butter
4 cups shredded Monterey Jack cheese

Sauté onion in a skillet in hot oil. Add ground beef, chili powder, ground cumin, salt, and garlic. When ground beef is brown, stir in tomato sauce. Heat through. Stir in black olives.

Prepare foil strips as directed on page 219. Place in any size Crock-Pot. Lightly butter one of corn tortillas. Lay one tortilla, buttered side up on foil strips. Spread with meat sauce and a layer of cheese. Cover with another tortilla, more meat sauce and cheese. Repeat layers ending with cheese. Cover; and cook on High 1 hour. When ready to serve lift out, using foil strips, and transfer to serving dish. Discard foil strips. Cut into wedges. Serve with sour cream and green onion if desired. *Serves 4 to 5.*

Each Serving:	Calories 1,396 kcal	Protein 71 gm
	Fat 106 gm	Carbohydrate 41 gm
	Sodium 2,433 mg	Cholesterol 313 mg

SWEET AND SOUR MEATBALLS OVER RICE

1 pound ground beef
1 egg, lightly beaten
4 tablespoons cornstarch, divided
1 teaspoon salt
¼ teaspoon black pepper
1 tablespoon dried chopped onion
1 tablespoon cooking oil
3 tablespoons vinegar
1 can (15 ounces) pineapple chunks
½ cup sugar
1 tablespoon soy sauce
1 large green pepper, cut into pieces
hot cooked rice

In a bowl, combine ground beef, egg, 1 tablespoon cornstarch, salt, pepper, and onion. Shape into 1½-inch balls. In a large skillet, lightly brown meatballs in oil. Drain fat from skillet. Transfer meatballs to any size Crock-Pot.

Stir together in a small bowl, vinegar, sugar, soy sauce, remaining cornstarch, and green pepper. Pour over meatballs. Cover and cook on Low 6 to 8 hours or on High 2 to 4 hours. In the last 30 minutes of cooking stir in the can of pineapple. Serve over hot cooked rice. *Serves 4 to 5.*

Variation: Substitute ground turkey for ground beef

Each Serving:	Calories 414 kcal	Protein 17 gm
	Fat 20 gm	Carbohydrate 42 gm
	Sodium 715 mg	Cholesterol 103 mg

BEEF STROGANOFF

1½   pounds stew meat, cut into 1-inch cubes
1   tablespoon cooking oil
1   jar (4 ounces) sliced mushrooms
1   tablespoon dried minced onion
2   cloves garlic, minced or ¼ teaspoon garlic powder
½   teaspoon dried crushed oregano
¼   teaspoon salt
¼   teaspoon black pepper
⅛   teaspoon dried crushed thyme
1   bay leaf
1½   cups beef broth
⅓   cup dry cooking sherry
1   carton (8 ounces) dairy sour cream
½   cup all-purpose flour
¼   cup water
4   cups hot cooked noodles or rice

In a large skillet brown beef in hot oil. Drain off fat.

In Crock-Pot combine beef, mushrooms, onions, garlic, oregano, salt, pepper, thyme, and bay leaf. Pour in beef broth and cooking sherry. Cover; cook on Low for 8 to 10 hours or on High for 4 to 5 hours. Discard bay leaf.

If using Low heat, turn to High heat. Mix together sour cream, flour, and water. Stir about 1 cup of the hot liquid into sour cream mixture. Return all to cooker; stir to combine. Cover and cook on High for 30 minutes or until thickened and bubbly. Serve over noodles or rice. *Serves 6.*

Each Serving: Calories 457 kcal   Protein 30 gm
                Fat 19 gm   Carbohydrate 39 gm
                Sodium 772 mg   Cholesterol 126 mg

SIMPLE BRISKET

4-5 pounds fresh beef brisket
1   envelope (1½ ounces) dry onion soup mix
1   can (4 ounces) mushrooms undrained

Trim all excess fat from brisket. Combine onion soup mix with mushrooms and their liquid. Place brisket in Crock-Pot with fat side up, cutting to fit if necessary. Spread onion soup mixture over top of brisket, moistening well. Cover and cook on Low for 10 to 14 hours.

Remove brisket and cut across the grain into thin slices. Serve with meat juices poured over top of slices. *Serves 8 to 10.*

Each Serving:	Calories 290 kcal	Protein 37 gm
	Fat 13 gm	Carbohydrate 3 gm
	Sodium 613 mg	Cholesterol 110 mg

HAMBURGER HOT POT

1½ pounds ground chuck or lean ground beef
¼   teaspoon garlic powder
1   teaspoon salt
¼   teaspoon pepper
6   medium potatoes, peeled and sliced
3   medium onions, sliced
1   can (10¾ ounces) condensed golden mushroom soup
½   cup water

In skillet, lightly brown ground beef; drain well. Add garlic powder, salt and pepper; set aside. Place half the potatoes and half the onions in greased Crock-Pot. Add browned beef. Top with remaining potatoes and onions. Combine mushroom soup and water; spread over top, being sure to moisten and cover evenly. Cover and cook on Low for 8 to 10 hours or on High for 3 to 4 hours. *Serves 4 to 6.*

Each Serving:	Calories 443 kcal	Protein 28 gm
	Fat 21 gm	Carbohydrate 35 gm
	Sodium 999 mg	Cholesterol 82 mg

 **FAVORITE BRISKET**

4 pounds fresh beef brisket
1 teaspoon salt
2 teaspoons dry mustard
2 teaspoons paprika
$\frac{1}{8}$ teaspoon pepper
$\frac{1}{2}$-1 teaspoon garlic powder

Trim all excess fat from brisket. Combine seasonings until well blended; rub into brisket. Place meat in Crock-Pot with fat side up, cutting to fit if necessary. Cover and cook on Low for 10 to 12 hours.

Remove brisket from liquid and cut across the grain into thin slices. Serve au jus. *Serves 6 to 8.*

Each Serving:	Calories 307 kcal	Protein 41 gm
	Fat 15 gm	Carbohydrate 1 gm
	Sodium 468 mg	Cholesterol 121 mg

LASAGNA WITH WHITE SAUCE

Try this Lasagna with a twist. We use a white sauce instead of the usual red sauce.

1   pound ground beef
1   onion, chopped
1   can (14$\frac{1}{2}$ ounces) diced tomatoes
2   tablespoons tomato paste
1   beef bouillon cube
1$\frac{1}{2}$ teaspoons Italian seasoning
1   teaspoon salt
$\frac{1}{2}$ teaspoon black pepper
$\frac{1}{4}$ teaspoon cayenne pepper
1   package (8 ounces) mini lasagna noodles, cooked and drained

White Sauce
2   tablespoons margarine or butter, melted
3   tablespoons all-purpose flour
1   teaspoon salt
$\frac{1}{4}$ teaspoon black pepper
2   cups milk
2   cups shredded mozzarella, divided

Cook lasagna noodles in boiling water for 5 minutes. Drain. In a skillet, brown ground beef and onion, until onion is tender. Drain fat. Transfer meat mixture to Crock-Pot. Stir in tomatoes, tomato paste, bouillon, and seasonings. Add cooked lasagna noodles. In a small bowl, mix melted margarine, flour, salt, pepper, milk, and 1 cup of mozzarella cheese. Stir into Crock-Pot. Cover and cook on Low 4 to 6 hours or on High 2 to 3 hours. In the last 30 minutes, turn Crock-Pot to High, if cooking on Low. Top with remainder of mozzarella cheese. Serve when cheese is melted. *Serves 10 to 12.*

Each Serving:	Calories 302 kcal	Protein 16 gm
	Fat 16 gm	Carbohydrate 23 gm
	Sodium 715 mg	Cholesterol 50 mg

BEEF N' BEAN BURRITOS

2   packages (1$\frac{1}{2}$ ounces each)
     enchilada sauce mix
3   cups water
1   can (12 ounces) tomato paste
$\frac{1}{4}$ teaspoon black pepper
$\frac{1}{8}$ teaspoon garlic powder
     salt to taste
2   pounds ground beef
5   large flour tortillas (9-inch)
4   cups shredded cheddar cheese
1   can (12 ounces) refried beans

Garnish with taco sauce, sour cream, salsa, chopped
onion, chili peppers, guacamole.

Lightly grease Crock-Pot. Prepare foil handles as described
on page 219. Place in Crock-Pot. In a saucepan, combine
the first six ingredients; simmer for 15 minutes over Low
heat. In a skillet, brown ground beef. Drain. Stir in $\frac{1}{3}$ of
sauce mix into browned beef. Spoon a small amount of
sauce into bottom of the Crock-Pot. Spread a small amount
of refried beans over flour tortilla. Place tortilla on top of
sauce in Crock-Pot, tearing to fit if necessary. Spoon meat
mixture over tortilla and then top with a small amount of
cheese. Continue layering process until the top of Crock-
Pot is reached, ending with a layer of cheese. Cover and
cook on Low 6 to 8 hours or on High for 3 to 4 hours. Lift
burritos out by the foil handles and place on serving plate.
Cut in wedges and garnish as desired. *Serves 4 to 6.*

Each Serving:	Calories 1,073 kcal	Protein 65 gm
	Fat 64 gm	Carbohydrate 60 gm
	Sodium 3,689 mg	Cholesterol 205 mg

RAVIOLI CASSEROLE

This flavorful casserole uses several favorite Italian ingredients.

1½   pounds ground beef
  1   medium onion, chopped
  1   clove garlic, minced or
       ⅛ teaspoon garlic powder
  2   cans (8 ounces each) tomato sauce
  1   can (14 ounces) stewed tomatoes
  1   teaspoon dried crushed oregano
  1   teaspoon Italian seasoning
       salt and pepper to taste
  1   package (10 ounces) frozen, chopped
       spinach, thawed
  1   package (16 ounces) bow-tie pasta, cooked
  ½   cup grated Parmesan cheese
1½   cups shredded mozzarella cheese

In a large skillet over medium-high heat, brown ground beef, onion, and garlic. Cook until onion becomes clear and soft, approximately 20 minutes. Drain excess fat. Transfer meat mixture to Crock-Pot.

Add the tomatoes, tomato sauce, oregano, Italian seasoning, and salt and pepper, stirring to break up stewed tomatoes. Cover and cook on Low for 7 to 8 hours or on High for 3½ to 4 hours. In the last 30 minutes turn to High if on Low. Stir in the cooked pasta, spinach, and cheese. Serve immediately when mozzarella cheese is melted. *Serves 6.*

Each Serving:	Calories 736 kcal	Protein 40 gm
	Fat 32 gm	Carbohydrate 72 gm
	Sodium 996 mg	Cholesterol 106 mg

SWEET AND SOUR BEEF OVER RICE

This is a delicious beef version of sweet-and-sour and is especially good when served over rice and noodles.

2	pounds boneless chuck
2/3	cup all-purpose flour
2	teaspoons salt
1/2	teaspoon black pepper
2	tablespoons margarine or butter
1	tablespoon olive oil
1	large onion, chopped
1/2	cup ketchup
1/4	cup brown sugar
1/4	cup red wine vinegar
1	tablespoon Worcestershire sauce
1	cup water
1	teaspoon salt
	pepper to taste
4-6	carrots diagonally sliced

Cut beef into 1-inch cubes. Mix together flour, salt, and pepper and dredge cubes in mixture. In a skillet, heat margarine and olive oil and brown beef cubes. Place browned beef in the Crock-Pot. Add remaining ingredients except for carrots. Cover and cook on Low for 8 to 9 hours or on High for 4 to 5 hours. Add carrots and cook on Low 1½ hours or on High for 30 minutes. Serve over rice. *Serves 6.*

Each Serving:	Calories 592 kcal	Protein 29 gm
	Fat 37 gm	Carbohydrate 35 gm
	Sodium 1,540 mg	Cholesterol 109 mg

AMERICA'S FAVORITE POT ROAST

3$\frac{1}{2}$-4	pounds beef arm or boneless pot roast
$\frac{1}{4}$	cup flour
2	teaspoons salt
$\frac{1}{8}$	teaspoon pepper
3	carrots, pared, sliced lengthwise and cut into 2-inch pieces
3	potatoes, peeled and quartered
2	small onions, sliced
1	stalk celery, cut into 2-inch pieces
1	jar (2 ounces) mushrooms, drained or $\frac{1}{4}$ cup mushroom gravy
3	tablespoons flour
$\frac{1}{4}$	cup water

Trim all excess fat from roast; brown and drain if using chuck or another highly marbled cut. Combine $\frac{1}{4}$ cup flour, the salt and pepper. Coat meat with the flour mixture. Place all vegetables except mushrooms in Crock-Pot and top with roast (cut roast in half, if necessary, to fit easily). Spread mushrooms evenly over top of roast. Cover and cook on Low for 10 to 12 hours.

If desired, turn to High during last hour to soften vegetables and make a gravy. To thicken gravy, make a smooth paste of the 3 tablespoons flour and the water and stir into Crock-Pot. Season to taste before serving. *Serves 4 to 6.*

Each Serving: Calories 582 kcal   Protein 76 gm
Fat 15 gm   Carbohydrate 31 gm
Sodium 1,163 mg   Cholesterol 204 mg

BAVARIAN POT ROAST

3-4	pounds beef arm pot roast
1	teaspoon vegetable oil
1	teaspoon salt
$\frac{1}{8}$	teaspoon pepper
$\frac{1}{2}$	teaspoon ground ginger
3	whole cloves
4	medium apples, cored and quartered
1	small onion, sliced
$\frac{1}{2}$	cup apple juice or water
3-4	tablespoons flour
3-4	tablespoons water

Wipe roast well and trim off excess fat. Lightly rub top of meat with oil. Dust with salt, pepper and ginger. Insert cloves in roast. Place apples and onions in Crock-Pot and top with roast (cut roast in half, if necessary, to fit easily). Pour in apple juice. Cover and cook on Low for 10 to 12 hours or on High for 5 to 6 hours.

Remove roast and apples to warm platter. Turn Crock-Pot to High setting. Make a smooth paste of the flour and water; stir into Crock-Pot. Cover and cook until thickened. *Serves 6 to 8.*

Each Serving:	Calories 377 kcal	Protein 49 gm
	Fat 11 gm	Carbohydrate 19 gm
	Sodium 468 mg	Cholesterol 136 mg

GLAZED CORNED BEEF

1	bay leaf
1	medium onion, sliced
2-3	strips of fresh orange peel (about 2 inches each)
3	whole cloves
1½	cups water
3-4	pounds corned beef (preferably round or rump cut)
	Glaze (below)

Combine all ingredients except corned beef and Glaze in Crock-Pot. Add corned beef with fat side up. Cover and cook on Low for 10 to 12 hours or until fork tender or on High for 5 to 6 hours.

Remove meat from broth. Score top of corned beef in diamond shapes. Insert additional cloves to decorate.

About 30 minutes before serving, place corned beef on heatproof platter. Prepare Glaze and spoon over corned beef. Bake in 375° oven for 20 to 30 minutes, basting occasionally with Glaze.

Glaze

3	tablespoons frozen orange juice concentrate, thawed
3	tablespoons honey
1	tablespoon Dijon-style mustard

Mix together until smooth and blended. *Serves 8 to 10.*

Each Serving:	Calories 348 kcal	Protein 23 gm
	Fat 24 gm	Carbohydrate 9 gm
	Sodium 1,454 mg	Cholesterol 122 mg

SAVORY PEPPER STEAK

1½-2 pounds beef round steak, about ½-inch
      thick
¼   cup flour
½   teaspoon salt
⅛   teaspoon pepper
1   medium onion, chopped
1   small clove garlic, minced
2   large green or red peppers, seeded and cut
      into ½-inch strips
1   can (16 ounces) whole tomatoes
1   tablespoon beef flavor base (paste or
      granules)
1   tablespoon soy sauce
2   teaspoons Worcestershire sauce
      Fluffy rice

Cut steak into strips. Combine ¼ cup flour, the salt and pepper; toss with steak strips to coat thoroughly. Add to Crock-Pot with onion, garlic and half of pepper strips; stir.

Combine tomatoes with beef base, soy sauce and Worcestershire sauce. Pour into Crock-Pot, moistening meat well. Cover and cook on Low for 8 to 10 hours.

One hour before serving, turn to High and stir in remaining green pepper strips. If thickened gravy is desired, make a smooth paste of 3 tablespoons flour and 3 tablespoons water; stir into Crock-Pot. Cover and cook until thickened. Serve gravy with Pepper Steak over hot fluffy rice. *Serves 4.*

Each Serving: Calories 494 kcal   Protein 44 gm
               Fat 26 gm   Carbohydrate 19 gm
               Sodium 1,481 mg   Cholesterol 125 mg

FLANK STEAK TERIYAKI

2   pounds beef flank steak

6   slices canned juice-pack pineapple
     (reserve 1/2 cup juice)

2   tablespoons soy sauce

1/2 teaspoon ground ginger

1   tablespoon dry sherry

2   tablespoons brown sugar

1   teaspoon Worcestershire sauce

2   chicken boullion cubes

1 1/2 cups boiling water

1   cup raw long-grain converted rice

Roll flank steak, tie and cut into 6 individual steaks. In
shallow bowl, stir together pineapple juice, soy sauce,
ginger, sherry, sugar and Worcestershire sauce. Marinate
steaks about 1 hour in soy mixture at room temperature.
Dissolve boullion cubes in boiling water; combine with
rice and 1/2 cup of soy mixture in Crock-Pot. Top each
steak with a pineapple ring, then place in Crock-Pot.
Cover and cook on Low for 8 to 10 hours or on High for
3 to 4 hours. *Serves 6.*

Each Serving:	Calories 439 kcal	Protein 33 gm
	Fat 16 gm	Carbohydrate 37 gm
	Sodium 784 mg	Cholesterol 79 gm

SMOTHERED FLANK STEAK

2½ pounds beef flank or round steak
   salt and pepper
1 tablespoon Worcestershire sauce
1 tablespoon vegetable oil
   paprika
2 medium onions, thinly sliced
½ pound mushrooms, sliced or 2 cans
   (4 ounces each) sliced mushrooms, drained
   chopped parsley

With sharp knife, score meat about ⅛-inch deep in diamond pattern on top side. Season with salt and pepper. Rub in Worcestershire sauce and oil. Sprinkle top with paprika. Place sliced onions and mushrooms in Crock-Pot. Roll flank steak, if necessary, to fit easily, and place on top of onions. Cover and cook on Low for 8 to 10 hours or on High for 4 to 5 hours.

Remove steak to warm carving platter and cut across the grain in thin diagonal slices. Serve with onions and mushrooms, pouring unthickened gravy over all. Sprinkle with parsley. *Serves 6.*

Each Serving:	Calories 394 kcal	Protein 39 gm
	Fat 23 gm	Carbohydrate 7 gm
	Sodium 1651 mg	Cholesterol 98 mg

BEEF, PORK AND LAMB

TACO BAKE

1   pound ground beef
1   onion, chopped
¾   cup water
1   package (1¼ ounces) taco seasoning
1   15 ounce can tomato sauce
2   cans (8 ounces each) tomato sauce
1   package (8 ounce) shell macaroni, uncooked
1   4 ounce can mild chopped green chilies
2   cups mild shredded cheddar cheese

In a skillet, brown ground beef and onion; drain fat. Add the water, taco seasoning and tomato sauce; mix. Simmer for 20 minutes. Transfer to Crock-Pot. Stir in macaroni and chopped green chilies. Cover and cook on Low for 6 to 8 hours or on High 3 to 4 hours. In the last 30 minutes of cooking top with shredded cheddar cheese. *Serves 6 to 8.*

Each Serving:	Calories 471 kcal	Protein 25 gm
	Fat 23 gm	Carbohydrate 39 gm
	Sodium 1,525 mg	Cholesterol 77 mg

BEEF ROULADES

1½   pounds beef round steak, ½ inch thick
4   slices bacon
¾   cup diced celery
¾   cup diced onion
½   cup diced green pepper
1   can (10 ounces) beef gravy

Cut steak into four serving pieces. Place bacon slice on each piece of meat. Mix celery, onion and green pepper;

place about ¹/₂ cup mixture on each piece of meat. Roll up meat; secure ends with wooden picks.

Wipe beef rolls with paper towels. Place in Crock-Pot. Pour gravy evenly over steaks to thoroughly moisten. Cover Crock-Pot and cook on Low for 8 to 10 hours or on High for 4 to 5 hours. Skim off fat before serving. *Serves 4.*

Each Serving:	Calories 417 kcal	Protein 43 gm
	Fat 23 gm	Carbohydrate 8 gm
	Sodium 309 mg	Cholesterol 116 mg

BEEF DIABLO

3-4 pounds beef arm or boneless pot roast
2-3 potatoes, peeled and sliced
1 onion, sliced
2 tablespoons flour
1 tablespoon prepared mustard
1 tablespoon chili sauce
1 tablespoon Worcestershire sauce
1 teaspoon vinegar
1 teaspoon sugar

Trim all excess fat from roast. Place potatoes and onion in bottom of Crock-Pot.

Make a smooth paste of flour, mustard, chili sauce, Worcestershire sauce, vinegar, and sugar. Spread over top of roast (cut roast in half, if necessary, to fit easily). Place roast in Crock-Pot on top of potatoes and onions. Cover and cook on Low for 10 to 12 hours or on High for 5 to 6 hours. *Serves 4 to 6 .*

Each Serving:	Calories 500 kcal	Protein 70 gm
	Fat 14 gm	Carbohydrate 19 gm
	Sodium 336 mg	Cholesterol 191 mg

BEEF, PORK AND LAMB

NORWEGIAN MEATBALLS IN SAUCE

1½ pounds extra-lean ground beef
½ pound extra-lean ground pork or veal
1 egg
1 cup mashed potatoes
½ cup dry bread crumbs
½ cup milk
1 teaspoon seasoned salt
¼ teaspoon ground cloves
¼ teaspoon allspice
¼ teaspoon ground ginger
¼ teaspoon black pepper
¼ teaspoon nutmeg
¼ teaspoon brown sugar
½ cup flour
1 cup beef broth
½ cup heavy cream
½ cup chopped parsley

Thoroughly combine all ingredients except flour, beef broth, heavy cream and chopped parsley. Blend well and shape into about twenty-four 1½ inch meatballs. Roll lightly in flour. Place on rack of broiler pan in preheated 400° oven for 20 minutes. Drain and place in Crock-Pot. Pour beef broth over meatballs. Cover and cook on Low for 7 to 9 hours or on High for 2 to 3 hours.

Before serving, carefully remove meatballs to warm platter. Stir heavy cream into broth in Crock-Pot; mix until smooth. Pour sauce over meatballs, then sprinkle with the chopped parsley. *Serves 6 to 8.*

Each Serving:	Calories 398 kcal	Protein 31 gm
	Fat 22 gm	Carbohydrate 20 gm
	Sodium 690 mg	Cholesterol 139 mg

CURRIED BEEF

3 pounds beef round steak or lean stewing beef, cut into 1½-inch cubes
½ cup flour
1 tablespoon curry powder
2 cloves garlic, minced
1 cup raisins
2 apples, peeled, cored and sliced
1 cup diced onion
1 teaspoon salt
½ teaspoon pepper
1 can (14 ounces) beef broth
2 apples (unpeeled), cored and finely chopped fluffy rice

Wipe beef well. Mix flour and curry powder. Coat meat cubes with flour mixture. Place meat in Crock-Pot. Add garlic, raisins, sliced apples, onion, salt and pepper. Pour in broth and stir to blend. Cover and cook on Low for 8 to 10 hours or on High for 4 to 5 hours; until meat is tender.

Before serving, stir in additional curry powder to taste (up to 1 tablespoon) and chopped apples. Serve over hot rice. *Serves 6 to 8.*

Note: Three pounds cubed lean lamb may be substituted for the beef.

Each Serving:	Calories 550 kcal	Protein 42 gm
	Fat 26 gm	Carbohydrate 37 gm
	Sodium 817 mg	Cholesterol 123 mg

ENGLISH BEEF POT PIE

2 **pounds beef round steak, cut into 1-inch cubes**
3 **tablespoons flour**
1 **teaspoon salt**
1/8 **teaspoon pepper**
2 **medium carrots, pared and sliced**
3 **medium potatoes, peeled and sliced**
1 **large onion, thinly sliced**
1 **can (16 ounces) whole tomatoes**
Biscuit Topping (below)

Place steak cubes in Crock-Pot. Combine flour, salt and pepper; toss with steak to coat thoroughly. Stir in remaining ingredients except Biscuit Topping and mix thoroughly. Cover and cook on Low for 8 to 10 hours or on High for 4 to 5 hours.

One hour before serving, remove meat and vegetables from Crock-Pot and pour into shallow 2½ quart baking dish. Preheat oven to 425°. Cover meat mixture with Biscuit Topping. Bake for 20 to 25 minutes. *Serves 4.*

Biscuit Topping
2 **cups flour**
1 **teaspoon salt**
3 **teaspoons baking powder**
1/4 **cup shortening**
3/4 **cup milk**

Mix dry ingredients. Cut in shortening until mixture resembles coarse cornmeal. Add milk all at one time; stir well. Pat out on floured board; roll out to cover baking dish.

Each Serving:	Calories 975 kcal	Protein 59 gm
	Fat 45 gm	Carbohydrate 83 gm
	Sodium 1,816 mg	Cholesterol 149 mg

SWISS STEAK

2 pounds beef round steak, about 1-inch thick
1/4 cup flour
1 teaspoon salt
1 stalk celery, chopped
2 carrots, pared and chopped
1/4 cup chopped onion
1/2 teaspoon Worcestershire sauce
1 can (8 ounces) tomato sauce
1/2 cup grated process American cheese
(optional)

Cut steak into 4 serving pieces. Dredge in flour mixed
with salt; place in Crock-Pot. Add chopped vegetables
and Worcestershire sauce. Pour tomato sauce over meat
and vegetables. Cover and cook on Low for 8 to 10 hours
or on High for 4 to 5 hours.

Just before serving, sprinkle with grated cheese. *Serves 4.*

Recipe may be doubled for 5-quart Crock-Pot. Cook the
maximum time.

Each Serving:	Calories 528 kcal	Protein 48 gm
	Fat 29 gm	Carbohydrate 15 gm
	Sodium 1,042 mg	Cholesterol 143 mg

BEEF TIPS

1/2   cup flour
1   teaspoon salt
1/8   teaspoon pepper
4   pounds beef or sirloin tips
1/2   cup chopped shallots or green onions
2   cans (4 ounces each) sliced mushrooms, drained, or 1/2 pound mushrooms, sliced
1   can (10 1/2 ounces) condensed beef broth
1   teaspoon Worcestershire sauce
2   teaspoons tomato paste or ketchup
1/4   cup dry red wine or water
3   tablespoons flour
    buttered noodles

Combine 1/2 cup flour with the salt and pepper and toss with beef cubes to coat thoroughly. Place in Crock-Pot. Add shallots and mushrooms. Combine beef broth, Worcestershire sauce and tomato paste. Pour over beef and vegetables; stir well. Cover and cook on Low for 8 to 12 hours or on High for 4 to 6 hours.

One hour before serving, turn to High setting. Make a smooth paste of red wine and 3 tablespoons flour; stir into Crock-Pot, mixing well. Cover and cook until thickened. Serve over hot buttered noodles. *Serves 8 to 10.*

Each Serving:	Calories 489 kcal	Protein 41 gm
	Fat 31 gm	Carbohydrate 10 gm
	Sodium 666 mg	Cholesterol 135 mg

HEARTY BEEF RAGOUT

3	pounds boneless beef chuck, cut into 1-inch pieces
$1/2$	cup flour
1	teaspoon salt
$1/4$	teaspoon pepper
1	package (8 ounces) precooked sausage links, cut into 1-inch pieces
2	cups chopped leeks
3-4	stalks celery, cut up
3	potatoes, peeled and cubed
1	can (16 ounces) whole tomatoes
1	teaspoon leaf oregano
2	cloves garlic, minced
$1/2$	cup beef broth
1	teaspoon Kitchen Bouquet
2	tablespoons flour
3	tablespoons water

Wipe beef well. Combine $1/3$ cup flour with salt and pepper. Toss beef cubes with flour mixture to coat thoroughly; place in Crock-Pot. Add remaining ingredients except 2 tablespoons flour and the water in order listed; stir well. Cover and cook on Low for 8 to 12 hours or on High for 4 to 6 hours.

One hour before serving, turn to High setting. Make a smooth paste of 2 tablespoons flour and the water; stir into Crock-Pot, mixing well. Cover and cook until thickened. *Serves 8.*

Each Serving:	Calories 643 kcal	Protein 36 gm
	Fat 45 gm	Carbohydrate 22 gm
	Sodium 837 mg	Cholesterol 141 mg

BRAISED SHORT RIBS

3-4 **pounds lean beef short ribs**
$1/2$ **cup flour**
$1^1/2$ **teaspoons paprika**
1 **teaspoon salt**
$1/2$ **teaspoon dry mustard**
2 **medium onions, sliced and separated into rings**
1 **clove garlic, chopped (optional)**
1 **cup beer, beef broth, or water**
2 **tablespoons flour (optional)**
3 **tablespoons water (optional)**

Place short ribs on broiler rack or in skillet and brown to remove fat; drain well. Combine $1/2$ cup flour with the paprika, salt and dry mustard; toss with short ribs. Place remaining ingredients except 2 tablespoons flour and the water in Crock-Pot; stir to mix beef ribs with onion rings (be sure onions are under beef ribs — not on top). Cover and cook on Low for 8 to 12 hours or on High for 4 to 6 hours.

Remove short ribs to warm serving platter. If thickened gravy is desired, make a smooth paste of flour and water. Turn Crock-Pot to High and stir in paste. Cover and cook until gravy is thickened. *Serves 6.*

Each Serving:	Calories 257 kcal	Protein 23 gm
	Fat 11 gm	Carbohydrate 15 gm
	Sodium 442 mg	Cholesterol 64 mg

MARINATED BARBECUE BRISKET

4-5 pounds fresh beef brisket
2 teaspoons unseasoned meat tenderizer
1/2 teaspoon celery salt
1/2 teaspoon seasoned salt
1/2 teaspoon garlic salt
1/4 cup liquid smoke
1/4 cup Worcestershire sauce
1 1/2 cups barbecue sauce

Place brisket on large piece of heavy-duty aluminum foil. Sprinkle tenderizer and seasonings on both sides of meat. Pour liquid smoke and Worcestershire sauce over top. Cover and marinate in refrigerator 6 to 10 hours or overnight.

Place foil-wrapped brisket in Crock-Pot (cut brisket in half, if necessary, to fit easily). Cover and cook on Low setting for 10 to 12 hours.

Chill brisket, then cut across the grain into thin slices. Before serving, reheat in your favorite barbecue sauce. *Serves 8 to 10.*

Each Serving:	Calories 677 kcal	Protein 40 gm
	Fat 53 gm	Carbohydrate 7 gm
	Sodium 1,107 mg	Cholesterol 156 mg

PEPPERED MEAT LOAF

2	pounds ground chuck
1/2	pound bulk sausage
1	large onion, finely chopped
3	cloves garlic, minced
1	can (8 ounces) tomato sauce
1/2	ketchup
3/4	cup crushed saltine crackers
2	eggs
2	teaspoons Worcestershire sauce
1	teaspoon seasoned salt
1/4	teaspoon seasoned pepper
1-2	potatoes, peeled and cut into fingers
	Sauce (below)

Combine all ingredients except potatoes and sauce; mix well and shape into a loaf. Place potatoes in bottom of Crock-Pot. Top potatoes with meat loaf. Pour sauce over all. Cover and cook on Low for 8 to 12 hours.
Serves 6 to 8.

Sauce

1	cup ketchup
1/3	cup brown sugar
1 1/2	teaspoons dry mustard
1/2	teaspoon nutmeg

Mix ingredients well.

Each Serving:	Calories 682 kcal	Protein 32 gm
	Fat 43 gm	Carbohydrate 41 gm
	Sodium 1,439 mg	Cholesterol 180 mg

SAUERBRATEN

4	pounds beef rump roast
1	cup dry rosé wine
¼	cup cider vinegar
3	large onions, sliced
2	stalks celery, sliced
1	clove garlic
2	whole allspice
3-4	whole cloves
1	teaspoon salt
½	teaspoon pepper
3	tablespoons flour
3	tablespoons water
1	cup crushed gingersnap cookies

Trim roast of all excess fat. In large bowl, combine all ingredients except roast, flour, water and gingersnaps; stir well. Place roast in marinade; refrigerate overnight.

Pour vegetable marinade into Crock-Pot. Place marinated roast in Crock-Pot with fat side up. Cover and cook on Low for 10 to 12 hours.

Thirty minutes before serving, remove roast and turn to High. Make a smooth paste of flour and water; stir into Crock-Pot with gingersnaps. Cook and stir until thickened. Slice roast and return to gravy for serving. *Serves 6 to 8.*

Each Serving:	Calories 476 kcal	Protein 59 gm
	Fat 16 gm	Carbohydrate 21 gm
	Sodium 557 mg	Cholesterol 153 mg

BEEF HASH

2-3 cups cut-up cooked beef
2 packages (10 ounces each) frozen hash brown potatoes, thawed
1 onion, finely chopped
1/4 cup butter or margarine, melted
1 cup gravy or beef broth
salt and pepper

Place all ingredients in Crock-Pot. Cover and cook on Low for 6 to 8 hours or on High for 2 to 3 hours. *Serves 4.*

Double recipe for 5-quart Crock-Pot.

Each Serving:	Calories 485 kcal	Protein 29 gm
	Fat 27 gm	Carbohydrate 32 gm
	Sodium 234 mg	Cholesterol 104 mg

CHOLENT

2-3 pounds frozen beef brisket
1 cup lima beans, completely softened (see page 162)
2 onions, sliced
1 cup water
1 teaspoon garlic salt
1/4 teaspoon coarsely ground pepper
1/4 teaspoon paprika

Trim all excess fat from brisket. Combine softened lima beans, onions and water in Crock-Pot; mix well. Add brisket and seasonings. Cover and cook on Low for 16 to

24 hours. Serve sliced meat over limas and onions with the natural juices over all. *Serves 4 to 6.*

Each Serving:	Calories 499 kcal	Protein 56 gm
	Fat 17 gm	Carbohydrate 29 gm
	Sodium 476 mg	Cholesterol 141 mg

MEATBALLS WITH GRAVY

1½ pounds ground beef
2 tablespoons chopped parsley flakes
1 teaspoon onion salt
¼ teaspoon garlic powder
¼ cup bread crumbs
¼ cup milk
1 egg
2 packages brown gravy mix

Combine first 7 ingredients to make 1-inch meatballs. Brown in a skillet. Drain fat. Place in a Crock-Pot. Cover. Cook on Low for 3 to 4 hours or can be kept on all day. When ready to serve prepare gravy mix as directed on the package and pour into meatballs. Stir. Serve over rice. *Serves 6.*

Each Serving:	Calories 332 kcal	Protein 22 gm
	Fat 23 gm	Carbohydrate 9 gm
	Sodium 728 mg	Cholesterol 114 mg

STUFFED CABBAGE

12	large cabbage leaves
1	pound lean ground beef or lamb
½	cup cooked rice
½	teaspoon salt
⅛	teaspoon pepper
¼	teaspoon leaf thyme
¼	teaspoon nutmeg
¼	teaspoon cinnamon
1	can (6 ounces) tomato paste
¾	cup water

Wash cabbage leaves. Boil 4 cups water. Turn heat off. Soak leaves in water for 5 minutes. Remove, drain, and cool.

Combine remaining ingredients except tomato paste and water. Place 2 tablespoons of mixture on each leaf and roll firmly. Stack in Crock-Pot. Combine tomato paste and water and pour over stuffed cabbage. Cover and cook on Low for 8 to 10 hours. *Serves 6.*

Each Serving:	Calories 274.83 kcal	Protein 16 gm
	Fat 16 gm	Carbohydrate 16 gm
	Sodium 479 mg	Cholesterol 57 mg

ZESTY MEATBALL SANDWICHES

1	egg
1/2	teaspoon salt
1/2	teaspoon Italian seasoning
1/4	teaspoon crushed red pepper flakes
2	cloves garlic, minced or 1/4 teaspoon garlic powder
1/4	cup chopped onion
1	pound ground beef
1	pound ground turkey
1/2	cup bread crumbs
1/3	cup grated Parmesan cheese
1	can (16 ounces) tomato sauce
2	tablespoons red wine vinegar
6-8	hoagie-type sandwich rolls, split and warmed

Condiments if desired: shredded mozzarella cheese, red and yellow pepper strips, sliced onion, olives.

In a large bowl, beat egg with salt, Italian seasoning, red pepper flakes, and garlic. Add chopped onion, beef, turkey, bread crumbs, and Parmesan cheese; mix well. Shape mixture into 1-inch balls and brown in a large skillet. Drain meatballs and transfer to a 5-quart Crock-Pot.

In the same bowl, mix tomato sauce and wine; pour over meatballs. Cover and cook on Low for 5 1/2 to 6 hours.

To serve, place 3 to 4 meatballs in each split roll; top with sauce from Crock-Pot. If desired add condiments and serve. *Serves 6 to 8.*

Each Serving:	Calories 522 kcal	Protein 32 gm
	Fat 24 gm	Carbohydrate 43 gm
	Sodium 1,164 mg	Cholesterol 121 mg

CAMP-OUT CHILI DOGS

1	pound frankfurters
1	large onion, finely chopped, or 3 tablespoons dried minced onion
2	cans (15 ounces each) chili with beans
1	teaspoon chili powder
1/4	pound cheddar cheese, cubed or grated frankfurter rolls

Combine all ingredients except cheese and rolls in Crock-Pot. Stir well. Cover and cook on Low for 5 to 10 hours or on High for 2 to 3 hours.

Add cheese just before serving and allow to melt slightly. Serve each frankfurter in a roll and spoon sauce over top. *Serves 6 to 8.*

Each Serving:	Calories 493 kcal	Protein 20 gm
	Fat 29 gm	Carbohydrate 39 gm
	Sodium 1,523 mg	Cholesterol 61 mg

CHOP SUEY

2-3	pork shoulder chops, boned, well trimmed and diced
2	cups cubed, cooked or raw chicken
1/2	cup chicken broth
1	cup diagonally sliced celery
2	teaspoons soy sauce
1/2	teaspoon sugar
	salt
1 1/2	cups water chestnuts, thinly sliced
1 1/2	cups bamboo shoots, in julienne strips

Combine all ingredients in Crock-Pot; stir well. Cover and cook on Low for 8 to 10 hours or on High for 4 to 5 hours. If desired, thicken sauce with a cornstarch-water paste just before serving. *Serves 4.*

Double recipe for 5-quart Crock-Pot.

Each Serving:	Calories 369 kcal	Protein 43 gm
	Fat 14 gm	Carbohydrate 16 gm
	Sodium 470 mg	Cholesterol 132 mg

SWEET AND SOUR PORK STEAKS

These pork steaks are delectably tangy and tender when prepared in the Crock-Pot.

4-6 pork shoulder steaks
1 tablespoon cooking oil
1 can (15 ounces) crushed pineapple
1/2 cup chopped green pepper
1/2 cup water
1/3 cup brown sugar
2 tablespoons ketchup
1 tablespoon quick-cooking tapioca
3 teaspoons soy sauce
1/2 teaspoon dry mustard

In a skillet brown pork steaks on both sides in hot oil. Drain fat. Transfer to any size Crock-Pot.

In a bowl, combine pineapple, green pepper, water, brown sugar, ketchup, tapioca, soy sauce, and dry mustard. Pour over pork steaks. Cover and cook on Low for 8 to 10 hours or on High 4 to 5 hours. Serve over rice if desired. *Serves 4 to 6.*

Each Serving:	Calories 496 kcal	Protein 22 gm
	Fat 31 gm	Carbohydrate 32 gm
	Sodium 368 mg	Cholesterol 102 mg

PORK CHOP AND POTATOES IN MUSTARD SAUCE

6-8   pork loin chops
2   tablespoons cooking oil
1   can (10¾ ounces) cream of mushroom soup
¼   cup chicken broth
¼   cup country Dijon-style mustard
½   teaspoon crushed dried thyme
1   clove garlic, minced or
    ¼ teaspoon garlic powder
¼   teaspoon black pepper
6   medium-sized potatoes cut into thin slices
1   onion, sliced

In a skillet brown pork chops on both sides in hot oil. Drain fat.

In any size Crock-Pot, mix cream of mushroom soup, chicken broth, mustard, thyme, garlic, and pepper. Add potatoes and onion, stirring to coat. Place browned pork chops on top of potato mixture. Cover and cook on Low for 8 to 10 hours or on High 4 to 5 hours. *Serves 6.*

Each Serving: Calories 448 kcal   Protein 28 gm
                 Fat 19 gm   Carbohydrate 37 gm
                 Sodium 767 mg   Cholesterol 73 mg

FRUIT AND HAM LOAF

3/4 cup dried fruit bits
2 tablespoons apple butter
1 beaten egg
1/4 cup milk
1/2 cup graham cracker crumbs
1/2 teaspoon black pepper
1 pound ground, fully cooked ham
1/2 pound ground pork
1/2 cup packed brown sugar
2 tablespoons apple juice
1/2 teaspoon dry mustard

In a small bowl combine fruit bits and apple butter. In a large bowl, combine egg, milk, graham cracker crumbs, pepper, ground ham, and ground pork.

Crisscross 3 foil strips as described on page 219 (atop a sheet of waxed paper to keep counter clean). In center of foil strips pat half of the meat mixture into a 7-inch circle. Spread fruit mixture on meat circle to within 1-inch of edges. Top with remaining meat mixture. Press edges of meat to seal well. Bringing up foil strips, lift and transfer to any size Crock-Pot. Press meat away from sides of Crock-Pot to avoid excess browning. Cover and cook on Low for 8 to 10 hours or on High for 4 to 6 hours. Loaf is done when meat thermometer inserted reads 170°.

In a small bowl combine brown sugar, apple juice, and dry mustard. Spread over meat. Cover and cook on Low or High heat for 30 minutes more.

Using foil strips, lift ham loaf from Crock-Pot and transfer to serving plate; discard foil strips. Serve. *Serves 6-8.*

Each Serving:	Calories 362 kcal	Protein 22 gm
	Fat 14 gm	Carbohydrate 36 gm
	Sodium 1,065 mg	Cholesterol 93 mg

CREAMY PORK WITH CORNMEAL BISCUITS

Cornmeal biscuits make a wonderful accompaniment to this Pork recipe.

1/4-1/2	cup onion, chopped
3	cloves garlic, minced or 3/4 teaspoon garlic powder
2	tart green apples, peeled, cored, and sliced
2	teaspoons sugar
1/2	teaspoon sage
1/4	teaspoon nutmeg
1/8	teaspoon white pepper
2-2 1/2	pounds boneless pork loin, trimmed and cut into 1-inch cubes
1/4	cup all-purpose flour
1/2	cup white cooking wine
1 1/2	tablespoons cornstarch
1/3	cup whipping cream
	salt to taste

In Crock-Pot, combine onion, garlic, apples, sugar, sage, nutmeg, and white pepper. Coat pork cubes with flour and then arrange over mixture in Crock-Pot. Pour in cooking wine. Cover and cook on Low 8 to 10 hours or on High 4 to 5 hours. Approximately 30 to 60 minutes before serving prepare the cornmeal biscuits as described below. While biscuits are baking, mix cornstarch and whipping cream in a small bowl. Pour into pork mixture and stir. Increase Crock-Pot to High if it has been cooking on Low. Continue to cook until sauce is hot and bubbly. Season to taste with salt. Serve with biscuits.

Cornmeal Biscuits

Preheat oven to 450°. In a large mixing bowl, stir together 1 1/2 cups all-purpose flour, 1/2 cup yellow cornmeal,

1 tablespoon baking powder, 1 teaspoon sugar, and ½ teaspoon salt. Dice ⅓ cup margarine; with a pastry blender or 2 knives, cut margarine into flour mixture until mixture resembles coarse crumbs. Add ¾ cup plain nonfat yogurt; stir just until mixture forms a sticky dough.

Form dough into a ball and knead on floured surface; then roll out to about ½-inch thick. Using a floured 2½-inch cutter, cut dough into 12 rounds.

Place 1 inch apart on an ungreased baking sheet. Bake in a 450° oven 10 to 12 minutes or until golden brown.

Serve hot with the Creamy Pork. *Serves 6 to 8.*

Each Serving:	Calories 535 kcal	Protein 37 gm
	Fat 22 gm	Carbohydrate 46 gm
	Sodium 670 mg	Cholesterol 102 mg

MEXICAN CARNITAS

1   pound lean boneless pork, cut into small cubes
1   package (10 ounces) frozen French style green beans, partially thawed
2   tablespoons minced onion
2   tablespoons chopped pimiento
½   teaspoon seasoned salt
⅛   teaspoon pepper

Place green beans in Crock-Pot. Top with onion, pimiento, seasoned salt and pepper; add cubed pork. Cover and cook on Low for 7 to 9 hours. *Serves 3 to 4.*

Double recipe for 5-quart Crock-Pot.

Each Serving:	Calories 202 kcal	Protein 23 gm
	Fat 9 gm	Carbohydrate 6 gm
	Sodium 520 mg	Cholesterol 76 mg

HAM TETRAZZINI

1   can (10³/₄ ounces) condensed cream of mushroom soup
¹/₂ cup evaporated or scalded milk
1¹/₂ teaspoons prepared horseradish
¹/₂ cup grated Romano or Parmesan cheese
1-1¹/₂ cups cubed cooked ham
¹/₂ cup stuffed olives, sliced (optional)
1   can (4 ounces) sliced mushrooms, drained
¹/₄ cup dry sherry or dry white wine
1   package (5 ounces) spaghetti
2   tablespoons butter, melted

Combine all ingredients except spaghetti and butter in Crock-Pot; stir well. Cover and cook on Low for 6 to 8 hours.

Just before serving, cook spaghetti according to package directions; drain and toss with butter. Stir into Crock-Pot. Sprinkle additional grated cheese over top. *Serves 4.*

This recipe may be doubled for the 5-quart Crock-Pot.

Each Serving: Calories 427 kcal   Protein 21 gm
                 Fat 21 gm   Carbohydrate 37 gm
                 Sodium 1,557 mg   Cholesterol 62 mg

STUFFED PORK CHOPS

4   double pork loin chops, well trimmed
     salt and pepper
1   can (12 ounces) whole-kernel corn, drained
1   small onion, chopped
1   small green pepper, seeded and chopped
1   cup fresh bread crumbs
1/2 teaspoon leaf oregano or leaf sage
1/3 cup raw, long-grain converted rice
1   can (8 ounces) tomato sauce

Cut a pocket in each chop, cutting from the edge almost
to the bone. Lightly season pockets with salt and pepper.
In bowl, combine all ingredients except pork chops and
tomato sauce. Pack vegetable mixture into pockets.
Secure along fat side with wooden picks.

Pour any remaining vegetable mixture into Crock-Pot.
Moisten top surface of each chop with tomato sauce.
Add stuffed pork chops to Crock-Pot, stacking to fit if
necessary. Pour any remaining tomato sauce on top.
Cover and cook on Low for 8 to 10 hours or on High for
4 to 5 hours; until done.

To serve, remove pork chops to heatproof platter and
mound vegetable-rice mixture in center. *Serves 4.*

Each Serving: Calories 346 kcal   Protein 29 gm
                Fat 7 gm   Carbohydrate 42 gm
                Sodium 690 mg   Cholesterol 66 mg

SPICY PORK AND CABBAGE

4-6   pork loin chops (about 1-inch thick), well trimmed
       salt and pepper
       Kitchen Bouquet
  4   cups coarsely shredded cabbage
3-4   tart apples, cored and diced
 1/2   small onion, chopped
  2   whole cloves
 1/2   small bay leaf
 1/4   cup sugar
  1   cup water
  2   tablespoons cider vinegar
  2   teaspoons salt

Season pork chops lightly with salt and pepper and brush with kitchen bouquet; set aside. Place cabbage, apples and onion in Crock-Pot. Add remaining ingredients except pork chops. Toss together well to evenly distribute spices. Arrange chops on top of cabbage mixture, stacking to fit. Cover and cook on Low for 8 to 10 hours or on High for 4 to 5 hours. *Serves 4 to 6.*

Each Serving:	Calories 274 kcal	Protein 25 gm
	Fat 7 gm	Carbohydrate 29 gm
	Sodium 949 mg	Cholesterol 66 mg

CANTONESE SWEET AND SOUR PORK

2   pounds lean pork shoulder, cut into strips
1   green pepper, seeded and cut into strips
1/2   medium onion, thinly sliced
1/4   cup brown sugar (packed)
2   tablespoons cornstarch
2   cups pineapple chunks (reserve juice)
1/4   cup cider vinegar
1/4   cup water
1   tablespoon soy sauce
1/2   teaspoon salt
      Chow mein noodles

Place pork strips in Crock-Pot. Add green pepper and sliced onion. In bowl, mix brown sugar and cornstarch. Add 1 cup reserved pineapple juice, the vinegar, water, soy sauce and salt; blend until smooth. Pour over meat and vegetables. Cover and cook on Low for 7 to 9 hours.

One hour before serving, add pineapple chunks; stir into meat and sauce.

Serve over chow mein noodles. *Serves 4 to 6.*

Each Serving:	Calories 407 kcal	Protein 36 gm
	Fat 14 gm	Carbohydrate 33 gm
	Sodium 569 mg	Cholesterol 122 mg

CANDIED POLYNESIAN SPARERIBS

2   pounds lean pork spareribs
1/3 cup soy sauce
1   tablespoon ground ginger
1/4 cup cornstarch
1/2 cup cider vinegar
1   cup sugar
1/4 cup water
1   teaspoon salt
1/2 teaspoon dry mustard
1   small piece gingerroot or crystallized ginger (about 1 inch)

Cut spareribs into individual 3-inch pieces. Mix soy sauce, ground ginger and cornstarch until smooth; brush mixture over spareribs. Place ribs on rack of broiler pan. Bake in preheated 425° oven for 20 minutes to remove fat; drain. Combine remaining ingredients in Crock-Pot; stir well. Add browned ribs. Cover and cook on Low for 8 to 10 hours or on High for 4 to 5 hours.

If desired, brown and crisp ribs in broiler for 10 minutes before serving. *Serves 4.*

Each Serving: Calories 599 kcal   Protein 27 gm
                   Fat 27 gm   Carbohydrate 62 gm
                   Sodium 1,993 mg   Cholesterol 107 mg

HONEY RIBS AND RICE

  2   pounds extra-lean back ribs
  1   can (10$\frac{1}{2}$ ounces) condensed beef consommé
$\frac{1}{2}$ cup water
  2   tablespoons maple syrup
  2   tablespoons honey
  3   tablespoons soy sauce
  2   tablespoons barbecue sauce
$\frac{1}{2}$ teaspoon dry mustard
1$\frac{1}{2}$ cups quick cooking rice

If ribs are fat, place on broiler rack and broil for 15 to 20 minutes; drain well. Otherwise, wash ribs and pat dry. Cut ribs into single servings. Combine remaining ingredients except rice in Crock-Pot; stir to mix. Add ribs. Cover and cook on Low for 8 to 10 hours or on High for 4 to 5 hours.

Remove ribs and keep warm. Turn Crock-Pot to High setting; add 1$\frac{1}{2}$ cups quick-cooking rice and cook until done.

Serve rice on warm platter surrounded by ribs. *Serves 4.*

Each Serving:	Calories 522 kcal	Protein 36 gm
	Fat 20 gm	Carbohydrate 48 gm
	Sodium 1,285 mg	Cholesterol 85 mg

BAKED HAM WITH MUSTARD GLAZE

3-5	pounds precooked ham, drained
10-12	whole cloves
1/2	cup brown sugar
1	tablespoon prepared mustard
2	teaspoons lemon juice
2	tablespoons orange juice
2	tablespoons cornstarch

Score ham in a diamond pattern and stud with cloves. Place in Crock-Pot. Combine brown sugar, mustard and lemon juice and spoon on ham. Cover and cook on High 1 hour, then on Low for 6 to 7 hours or until ham is hot.

Remove ham to warm serving platter. Turn Crock-Pot to High setting. Combine orange juice and cornstarch to form a smooth paste. Stir into drippings in Crock-Pot. Cook stirring occasionally until sauce is thickened. Spoon over ham.

5 or 6 quart unit: If cooking larger ham, cook 1 hour on High, then Low 8 to 10 hours. *Serves 12 to 15.*

Each Serving:	Calories 272 kcal	Protein 23 gm
	Fat 14 gm	Carbohydrate 13 gm
	Sodium 1,726 mg	Cholesterol 74 mg

HAM AND CHEESE SUPPER

2	cups ground cooked ham (about ½ pound)
½	cup finely crushed cheese crackers
1	egg
⅓	cup barbecue sauce
4	large potatoes, peeled and thinly sliced
1	medium onion, thinly sliced
2	tablespoons butter
2	tablespoons vegetable oil
⅔	cup evaporated milk
1	cup grated mozzarella cheese
1	teaspoon salt
¼	teaspoon paprika
⅛	teaspoon pepper

Combine ground ham, crushed crackers, egg and barbecue sauce and shape into 6 patties. In a skillet, sauté potato and onion slices in butter and oil over medium heat, turning frequently to prevent browning. Drain and place in Crock-Pot.

Combine milk, cheese and seasonings and pour over potatoes and onions. Layer ham patties on top. Cover and cook on Low for 3 to 5 hours. *Serves 6.*

Each Serving:	Calories 387 kcal	Protein 19 gm
	Fat 20 gm	Carbohydrate 32 gm
	Sodium 1,263 mg	Cholesterol 91 mg

STUFFED LAMB SHOULDER

3-4	pounds lamb shoulder, boned
1/2	pound bulk sausage
1	medium onion, chopped
1	tablespoon dried parsley flakes
1/2	teaspoon leaf marjoram
1/2	teaspoon leaf basil
1/2	teaspoon leaf oregano
1	clove garlic, minced (optional)
1	onion, sliced
2	stalks celery, sliced
2	carrots, pared and sliced
	Kitchen Bouquet
	salt and pepper

Trim all excess fat from lamb shoulder. To prepare stuffing, brown sausage and chopped onion in skillet; drain well. Stir in herbs and garlic. Stuff lamb with mixture. Roll lamb and fasten with skewers or string. Place sliced onion, celery and carrots in Crock-Pot. Place stuffed and rolled lamb on top of vegetables. Rub top of lamb with kitchen bouquet; sprinkle with salt and pepper. Cover and cook on High for 1 hour, then turn to Low for 10 to 12 hours.

Serve lamb sliced, with the natural juices poured over vegetables and meat. *Serves 6 to 8.*

Each Serving:	Calories 339 kcal	Protein 31 gm
	Fat 18 gm	Carbohydrate 10 gm
	Sodium 333 mg	Cholesterol 109 mg

LAMB CHOPS WITH ORANGE SAUCE

8   lamb rib chops
2   tablespoons vegetable oil
$\frac{1}{2}$ cup orange juice
2   tablespoons honey
2   teaspoons salt
2   tablespoons cornstarch
1   teaspoon grated orange peel

In skillet, brown lamb chops in oil; drain well.
Thoroughly combine orange juice, honey, salt, cornstarch
and grated orange peel. Brush browned lamb chops with
orange mixture and place in Crock-Pot. Cover and cook
on Low for 6 to 8 hours.

If a thicker sauce is desired, remove chops before serving
and turn Crock-Pot to High setting; stir in a mixture of 2
tablespoons cornstarch and $\frac{1}{4}$ cup water. Cook, stirring,
until the sauce is transparent. *Serves 4.*

Each Serving: Calories 865 kcal   Protein 30 gm
               Fat 75 gm   Carbohydrate 16 gm
               Sodium 1,218 mg   Cholesterol 158 mg

LAMB SHANKS WITH SPLIT PEAS

1	cup dried split green peas
3	pounds lamb shanks
1	large onion, chopped
2	carrots, pared and sliced
2	stalks celery, sliced
2½	cups beef broth
	salt and pepper

Completely soften peas as directed on page 162. Brown lamb shanks under broiler to remove fat; drain well. Mix all ingredients except shanks in Crock-Pot; stir well. Add shanks, pushing down into liquid. Cover and cook on Low for 10 to 12 hours. *Serves 4 to 6.*

Each Serving:	Calories 400 kcal	Protein 47 gm
	Fat 9 gm	Carbohydrate 31 gm
	Sodium 959 mg	Cholesterol 112 mg

POULTRY

CHEESY CHICKEN QUICHE

2   tablespoons corn oil
2   pounds chicken breasts, boneless and skinless
¾   cup flour
¾   teaspoon baking powder
½   teaspoon salt
1   cup evaporated milk
2   eggs, beaten
1   cup shredded cheddar cheese
2   tablespoons chopped onion
2   teaspoons dried parsley flakes

Coat Crock-Pot with corn oil. Cook chicken on Low 6 to 8 hours or on High 3 to 4 hours or until fork tender. Stir together flour, baking powder, salt, milk, and eggs. The cheese, onion, and parsley is then folded in. Pour mixture over chicken and cook 1 hour on High. *Serves approximately 6.*

Variation: cook with chicken, 1 package (10 ounces) frozen chopped, thawed broccoli. Then pour in cheese, flour and egg mixture.

Each Serving:	Calories 423 kcal	Protein 46 gm
	Fat 18 gm	Carbohydrate 17 gm
	Sodium 525 mg	Cholesterol 191 mg

CREAMY CHICKEN AND HAM MEDLEY

1   can (4 ounces) sliced mushrooms, drained
⅓   cup margarine or butter
⅓   cup all-purpose flour
2½ cups milk
1   cup grated Parmesan cheese
½   teaspoon salt
¼   teaspoon black pepper
¼   teaspoon nutmeg
    dash of ground red pepper
2   cups chopped cooked chicken
2   cups chopped cooked ham
2   packages (10 ounces each) frozen puff pastry
    shells, baked
    paprika

Melt margarine in Crock-Pot; stir in flour. Stir in
remaining ingredients with the exception of pastry shells
and paprika. Cook on Low until thickened, stirring after
every hour. Ready to serve after 2½ hours.

Bake pastry shells as directed on package. Spoon chicken
and ham medley into pastry shells and sprinkle with
paprika. Serve immediately.

Each Serving:	Calories 467 kcal	Protein 30 gm
	Fat 31 gm	Carbohydrate 27 gm
	Sodium 809 mg	Cholesterol 47 mg

SWISS CHICKEN CASSEROLE

6 chicken breasts, boneless and skinless
6 slices (4 x 4-inch) Swiss cheese
1 can (10¾ ounces) cream of mushroom soup, undiluted
¼ cup milk
2 cups herb stuffing mix
½ cup margarine or butter, melted

Spray Crock-Pot with cooking spray. Arrange chicken breasts in Crock-Pot. Top with cheese, layering cheese if necessary. Combine soup and milk; stir well. Spoon over cheese; sprinkle with stuffing mix. Drizzle melted margarine over stuffing mix. Cook on Low 8 to 10 hours or on High 4 to 6 hours. *Serves 6.*

Each Serving:	Calories 524 kcal	Protein 39 gm
	Fat 30 gm	Carbohydrate 23 gm
	Sodium 1,083 mg	Cholesterol 96 mg

CHICKEN STUFFING

1 chicken stuffing mix (12 serving size)
3-4 cups cooked, cubed chicken
3 cans (10¾ ounces each) cream of chicken soup
½ cup milk
2 cups shredded mild cheddar cheese

Prepare stuffing mix according to package directions and place in 5-quart Crock-Pot. Stir in 2 cans of cream of chicken soup. In a mixing bowl, stir together cubed chicken, 1 can cream of chicken soup and milk. Spread over stuffing in Crock-Pot. Sprinkle cheese over top. Cover and cook on Low 4 to 6 hours or on High 2 to 3 hours. *Serves 8 to 10.*

Each Serving: Calories 499 kcal   Protein 28 gm
              Fat 27 gm   Carbohydrate 33 gm
              Sodium 1,378 mg   Cholesterol 109 mg

CHICKEN PARMESAN

1	package onion soup mix
2	cans (10¾ ounces each) cream of mushroom soup, undiluted
1½	cup milk
1	cup white cooking wine
1	cup uncooked converted white rice
6	chicken breasts, boneless and skinless
6	tablespoons margarine or butter
	salt to taste
	pepper to taste
	grated Parmesan cheese

Mix onion soup mix, cream of mushroom soup, milk, cooking wine, and rice in a small mixing bowl. Spray Crock-Pot with cooking spray. Lay chicken breasts in Crock-Pot. Place one tablespoon margarine on each chicken breast. Pour soup mixture over chicken breasts. Salt and pepper to taste. Sprinkle with grated Parmesan cheese. Cook on Low 8 to 10 hours or on High for 4 to 6 hours. *Serves 6.*

Each Serving: Calories 539 kcal   Protein 34 gm
              Fat 24 gm   Carbohydrate 46 gm
              Sodium 1,890 mg   Cholesterol 78 mg

CHICKEN ENCHILADAS

2-3 pounds chopped cooked chicken
1 can (4$\frac{1}{2}$ ounces) chopped mild green chilies
1 onion, chopped
   Mexican Gravy, see recipe below
4 ounces shredded Monterey Jack cheese
4 ounces shredded mild or sharp cheddar cheese
1 can (4 ounces) chopped black olives
8 corn tortillas

In mixing bowl, stir together chicken, chilies, onion and 1 cup of Mexican gravy.

In Crock-Pot, place foil handles (see directions below). Dip tortilla in Mexican gravy and lay in Crock-Pot. Spread about 3 tablespoons chicken filling over tortilla, and sprinkle with cheese and olives. Continue layering process until the top of Crock-Pot has been reached. Final layer should be cheese and olive layer. Pour any excess gravy over top of tortilla stack. Cook on Low 4 to 6 hours or on High for 1$\frac{1}{2}$ to 2$\frac{1}{2}$ hours.

Mexican Gravy
$\frac{1}{2}$ stick margarine or butter
$\frac{1}{2}$ cup chili powder
$\frac{1}{3}$ cup flour
$\frac{1}{2}$ teaspoon garlic salt
$\frac{1}{4}$ teaspoon ground cumin
$\frac{1}{4}$ teaspoon crushed oregano
3 cans (15 ounces each) chicken broth
1 can (12 ounces) tomato sauce

Melt margarine in saucepan. In a bowl, mix together dry

ingredients. Slowly add dry ingredients to margarine, stirring constantly. Mixture will become crumbly. Slowly add chicken broth to margarine mixture, stirring constantly. Stir into tomato sauce.

Foil handles: tear off three 18 x 2-inch strips of heavy foil or use regular foil folded to double thickness. Crisscross the foil strips in a spoke design and place in Crock-Pot to make lifting of tortilla stack easier.

Each Serving:	Calories 790 kcal	Protein 71 gm
	Fat 41 gm	Carbohydrate 36 gm
	Sodium 2,292 mg	Cholesterol 208 mg

COOKED CHICKEN

Chicken can be prepared ahead of time for use in casseroles and other dishes.

2-3   **pounds chicken breasts or parts**
4   **cups water**
2   **tablespoon chopped parsley**
2   **teaspoons garlic powder**
1   **bay leaf**
1   **tablespoon minced onion**
1   **teaspoon seasoning salt**

Place all ingredients in Crock-Pot. Cook on Low 6 to 8 hours or on High for 3 to 4 hours.

Remove chicken from water, debone and skin if necessary. Discard bay leaf. Chop chicken meat for use in casseroles or other dishes.

Each Serving:	Calories 265 kcal	Protein 32 gm
	Fat 14 gm	Carbohydrate 1 gm
	Sodium 307 mg	Cholesterol 97 mg

LEMON HERBED ROASTED CHICKEN

3-4 pound fryer or roasting chicken
¼ cup chopped onion
2 tablespoons butter or margarine
  juice of one lemon
½ teaspoon salt
1 tablespoon fresh parsley (or 1 teaspoon dried parsley flakes)
¼ teaspoon leaf thyme
¼ teaspoon paprika

Rinse chicken well and pat dry; remove any excess fat. Place onion in the cavity of the chicken and rub the skin with butter or margarine. Place chicken in Crock-Pot. Squeeze the juice of the lemon over the chicken and sprinkle with remaining seasonings. Cover and cook on Low 8 to 10 hours or on High for 4 to 5 hours.

Each Serving:	Calories 317 kcal	Protein 32 gm
	Fat 20 gm	Carbohydrate 1 gm
	Sodium 318 mg	Cholesterol 113 mg

"FRIED" CHICKEN

2½-3 pound fryer, cut into serving pieces
1 cup flour
1 teaspoon salt
⅛ teaspoon freshly ground pepper
¼ teaspoon garlic powder
1 teaspoon paprika
1 teaspoon leaf sage or oregano
  butter or vegetable oil

Rinse chicken pieces and pat dry. Combine flour with remaining ingredients except butter. Toss chicken pieces with flour mixture to coat. In skillet, heat butter to ¼-inch depth and cook chicken over medium-high heat until golden brown. Place browned chicken in Crock-Pot, adding wings first; add no liquid. Cover and cook on Low for 8 to 10 hours or on High for 4 to 5 hours. *Serves 4.*

Each Serving:	Calories 496 kcal	Protein 41 gm
	Fat 25 gm	Carbohydrate 24 gm
	Sodium 722 mg	Cholesterol 137 mg

CHICKEN 'N OLIVES

3	pound fryer, cut into serving pieces
	salt and pepper
1	clove garlic, minced
1	large onion, chopped
2	bay leaves
¾	cup beer
1	can (8 ounces) tomato sauce
½	cup pimiento-stuffed olives
	fluffy rice

Rinse chicken pieces and pat dry. Lightly season with salt and pepper. Combine all ingredients except chicken and rice in Crock-Pot; stir well. Add chicken pieces, coating well; be sure all chicken is moistened. Cover and cook on Low for 7 to 9 hours. *Serves 4 to 6.*

Each Serving:	Calories 453 kcal	Protein 36 gm
	Fat 30 gm	Carbohydrate 9 gm
	Sodium 734 mg	Cholesterol 139 mg

TERIYAKI CHICKEN

2   pounds chicken breast, boneless and skinless
1   package (16 ounces) frozen broccoli, carrots, and water chestnuts
2   tablespoons quick-cooking tapioca
1   cup chicken broth
4   tablespoons brown sugar
4   tablespoons teriyaki sauce
2   tablespoons dry mustard
1½   teaspoons grated orange peel
1   teaspoon ground ginger
     hot cooked rice

Rinse chicken and pat dry. Cut chicken into 1-inch pieces. In Crock-Pot place frozen vegetables. Sprinkle with tapioca. Place chicken pieces on top of vegetables. In a small bowl, mix chicken broth, brown sugar, teriyaki sauce, mustard, orange peel, and ginger. Pour sauce over chicken pieces. Cover; cook on Low for 4 to 6 hours or on High for 2 to 3 hours. Serve over hot cooked rice.

Each Serving:	Calories 402 kcal	Protein 57 gm
	Fat 5 gm	Carbohydrate 31 gm
	Sodium 1,150 mg	Cholesterol 132 mg

CHICKEN SPECTACULAR

3   cups cut-up cooked chicken
1   can (16 ounces) cut green beans or peas, drained
2   cups cooked rice
1   can (10¾ ounces) condensed cream of celery soup

$^1\!/_2$ cup mayonnaise
1   can (6 or $8^1\!/_2$ ounces) water chestnuts,
    drained and sliced
2   tablespoons chopped pimiento
2   tablespoons finely chopped onion

Combine all ingredients thoroughly. Pour into greased
Crock-Pot. Cover and cook on Low for 6 to 8 hours or on
High for 3 to 4 hours. *Serves 4.*

Each Serving:	Calories 622 kcal	Protein 36 gm
	Fat 33 gm	Carbohydrate 44 gm
	Sodium 1,001 mg	Cholesterol 118 mg

CHICKEN 'N RICE
IN A BAG

3   pound fryer, cut into serving pieces
1   cup raw long-grain converted rice
1   can ($10^3\!/_4$ ounces) condensed cream of
    chicken soup
$^2\!/_3$ cup water
1   envelope ($1^1\!/_2$ ounces) dry onion soup mix

Rinse chicken pieces and pat dry; set aside. Combine
rice, cream of chicken soup and water in Crock-Pot; stir
well to mix in soup. Place chicken pieces in a see-
through roasting bag; add onion soup mix. Shake bag to
coat chicken pieces thoroughly. Puncture 4 to 6 holes in
bottom of bag. Fold top of bag over chicken and place in
Crock-Pot on top of rice. Cover and cook on Low for 8 to
10 hours or on High 4 to 5 hours. Remove chicken pieces
to warm platter. Serve with rice. *Serves 4.*

Each Serving:	Calories 772 kcal	Protein 50 gm
	Fat 40 gm	Carbohydrate 49 gm
	Sodium 1,716 mg	Cholesterol 180 mg

INTERNATIONAL CHICKEN

3	pound fryer, cut into serving pieces
1/4	cup flour
2	teaspoons salt
2	teaspoons curry powder
1/8	teaspoon pepper
1	large onion, chopped
1	large green pepper, seeded and sliced into rings
2	cloves garlic, minced
1/2	cup raisins
1	can (16 ounces) whole tomatoes, mashed
3	tablespoons flour
3	tablespoons water

Rinse chicken and pat dry. Combine 1/4 cup flour, the salt, curry powder and pepper. Dust chicken well with flour mixture. Place coated chicken in Crock-Pot and mix in chopped vegetables, garlic and raisins. Pour tomatoes over all. Cover and cook on Low for 8 to 10 hours or on High for 3 to 4 hours.

Remove chicken pieces to warm platter. Thicken sauce before serving by stirring a smooth paste of the 3 tablespoons flour and water into the sauce in Crock-Pot. Cover and cook on High until sauce is thickened. This is good served on rice — especially saffron rice. Spoon sauce over top. *Serves 4.*

Each Serving:	Calories 659 kcal	Protein 47 gm
	Fat 36 gm	Carbohydrate 37 gm
	Sodium 1,453 mg	Cholesterol 174 mg

CHICKEN FRICASSEE

3-4 pound stewing chicken or fryer, cut into serving pieces
2 teaspoons salt
1 teaspoon paprika
2 medium onions, sliced
3 stalks celery, sliced
2 carrots, pared and sliced
1 bay leaf
1 cup chicken broth
½ cup flour
½ cup water
1 package (10 ounces) noodles, cooked and drained
chopped parsley

Rinse chicken and pat dry. Season with salt and paprika. Place sliced vegetables and bay leaf in Crock-Pot. Place chicken pieces on top of vegetables. Pour in chicken broth. Cover and cook on Low for 8 to 12 hours or on High for 4 to 6 hours.

One hour before serving, turn to High. Remove chicken pieces; bone and return meat to Crock-Pot. Make a smooth paste of flour and water and stir into liquid in Crock-Pot. Cover and cook until thickened.

Serve over hot noodles; sprinkle with chopped parsley. *Serves 6 to 8.*

Each Serving:	Calories 352 kcal	Protein 31 gm
	Fat 6 gm	Carbohydrate 43 gm
	Sodium 888 mg	Cholesterol 115 mg

CHICKEN CHOW MEIN

4	pound hen or fryer, cut up
2	cups water
2	large white onions, chopped
2	cups diagonally sliced celery
1/4	cup flour or cornstarch
1/4	cup soy sauce
1	can (16 ounces) bean sprouts, drained
1	can (5 or 6 ounces) bamboo shoots (optional)
1	can (6 or 8 1/2 ounces) water chestnuts, drained and sliced
3	tablespoons molasses
	chow mein noodles or fluffy rice
	toasted slivered almonds

Place chicken with water, onions and celery in Crock-Pot. Cover and cook on Low for 8 to 10 hours.

One hour before serving, turn to High. Remove chicken; bone and cut up meat into bite-size pieces. Return to Crock-Pot. Combine flour with soy sauce and stir into Crock-Pot with bean sprouts, bamboo shoots, water chestnuts and molasses. Stir well until thickened. Taste for seasoning. Turn to Low until ready to serve, up to 4 hours.

Serve over chow mein noodles or hot fluffy rice. Sprinkle with toasted slivered almonds. *Serves 8 to 10.*

Each Serving:	Calories 366 kcal	Protein 28 gm
	Fat 21 gm	Carbohydrate 16 gm
	Sodium 598 mg	Cholesterol 103 mg

ALMOND CHICKEN

1	can (14 ounces) chicken broth
1	slice bacon, diced
2	tablespoons butter
¾-1	pound boned chicken breasts, cut into 1-inch pieces
1½	cups diagonally sliced celery
1	small onion, sliced
1	can (4 ounces) sliced mushrooms, drained
2	tablespoons soy sauce
½	teaspoon salt
	fluffy rice
⅔	cup slivered almonds, toasted

Pour chicken broth into Crock-Pot. Cover and turn Crock-Pot to High while browning meats and vegetables.

In skillet, heat bacon and butter; add chicken pieces and brown quickly on all sides. With slotted spoon, remove browned chicken to Crock-Pot. Quickly sauté celery, onion and mushrooms in skillet until just slightly limp.

Add contents of skillet to Crock-Pot with soy sauce and salt; stir well. Cover and cook on Low for 6 to 8 hours or on High for 3 to 4 hours.

Serve over hot fluffy rice and garnish with toasted almonds. *Serves 4.*

Each Serving:	Calories 365 kcal	Protein 30 gm
	Fat 23 gm	Carbohydrate 10 gm
	Sodium 1,481 mg	Cholesterol 77 mg

CHICKEN BREASTS
Á L'ORANGE

3	whole chicken breasts, halved
⅔	cup flour
1	teaspoon salt
1	teaspoon nutmeg
½	teaspoon cinnamon
	dash pepper
	dash garlic powder
2-3	sweet potatoes, peeled and cut into ¼-inch slices
1	can (10¾ ounces) condensed cream of celery or cream of chicken soup
1	can (4 ounces) sliced mushrooms, drained
½	cup orange juice
½	teaspoon grated orange rind
2	teaspoons brown sugar
3	tablespoons flour
	buttered rice

Rinse chicken breasts and pat dry. Combine ⅔ cup flour with salt, nutmeg, cinnamon, pepper and garlic powder. Thoroughly coat chicken in flour mixture.

Place sweet potato slices in bottom of Crock-Pot. Place chicken breasts on top.

Combine soup with remaining ingredients except buttered rice; stir well. Pour soup mixture over chicken breasts. Cover and cook on Low for 8 to 10 hours or on High for 3 to 4 hours or until chicken and vegetables are tender.

Serve chicken and sauce over hot buttered rice. *Serves 6.*

Each Serving:	Calories 443 kcal	Protein 34 gm
	Fat 16 gm	Carbohydrate 38 gm
	Sodium 897 mg	Cholesterol 98 mg

CHICKEN LICKIN'

6-8	chicken legs, thighs or breasts
3	tablespoons butter or margarine
1	large onion, chopped
1	clove garlic, minced
1	teaspoon salt
2	teaspoons paprika
½	teaspoon ground ginger
½	teaspoon chili powder
1	can (16 ounces) whole tomatoes
1	can (4 ounces) sliced mushrooms, drained
½	cup heavy cream (optional)

Rinse chicken parts and pat dry. In skillet, melt butter and brown chicken quickly on both sides. Place chicken in Crock-Pot. Stir together remaining ingredients except cream and pour over chicken. Cover and cook on Low for 8 to 10 hours or on High 4 to 5 hours. Just before serving, stir in heavy cream. Serve over hot spaghetti. *Serves 6 to 8.*

Each Serving:	Calories 298 kcal	Protein 28 gm
	Fat 17 gm	Carbohydrate 7 gm
	Sodium 593 mg	Cholesterol 96 mg

SOUPER CHICKEN

2	pounds chicken parts
1	can (10¾ ounces) condensed cream of celery soup
¼	cup flour
2	medium zucchini, cut lengthwise, then sliced diagonally into ½-inch pieces
1	teaspoon paprika
½	teaspoon leaf basil
1	clove garlic, minced
1	cup drained canned tomato wedges

Rinse chicken parts and pat dry. Mix celery soup with flour. Combine all ingredients in Crock-Pot; stir thoroughly to coat chicken. Cover and cook on Low for 8 to 10 hours or on High 4 to 5 hours. *Serves 4.*

Each Serving:	Calories 442 kcal	Protein 32 gm
	Fat 27 gm	Carbohydrate 17 gm
	Sodium 786 mg	Cholesterol 124 mg

BAKED CHICKEN BREASTS

2-3	whole chicken breasts, halved
2	tablespoons butter or margarine, melted
1	can (10¾ ounces) condensed cream of chicken soup
½	cup dry sherry
1	teaspoon leaf tarragon or leaf rosemary
1	teaspoon Worcestershire sauce

$^1/_4$ teaspoon garlic powder
1 can (4 ounces) sliced mushrooms, drained

Rise chicken breasts and pat dry; place in Crock-Pot.
Combine remaining ingredients and pour over chicken
breasts. Cover and cook on Low for 8 to 10 hours or on
High 4 to 5 hours. *Serves 4 to 6.*

Each Serving:	Calories 356 kcal	Protein 32 gm
	Fat 22 gm	Carbohydrate 7 gm
	Sodium 683 mg	Cholesterol 110 mg

CHICKEN CURRY

2 whole chicken breasts, boned
1 can (10$^3/_4$ ounces) cream of chicken soup
$^1/_4$ cup dry sherry
2 tablespoons butter or margarine
2 green onions with tops, finely chopped
1 teaspoon curry powder
1 teaspoon salt
   dash pepper
   fluffy rice or saffron rice

Cut chicken into small pieces; place in Crock-Pot. Add all
remaining ingredients except rice. Cover and cook on
High 2$^1/_2$ to 4 hours or on Low 6 to 8 hours. Serve over
hot rice. *Serves 4.* Double recipe for 5 quart Crock-Pot.

Each Serving:	Calories 378 kcal	Protein 33 gm
	Fat 24 gm	Carbohydrate 7 gm
	Sodium 1,302 mg	Cholesterol 114 mg

CHICKEN IN WINE

3   pounds chicken parts, preferably breasts
     and thighs
     salt and pepper
2   tablespoons butter
1   medium onion, sliced
1   can (4 ounces) sliced mushrooms, drained
1/2 cup dry sherry
1   teaspoon Italian seasoning
     fluffy rice

Rinse chicken parts and pat dry. Season chicken lightly
with salt and pepper. In skillet, melt butter and quickly
brown chicken parts; remove with slotted spoon and
place in Crock-Pot. Sauté onion and mushrooms in skillet.
Add sherry to skillet and stir, scraping to remove brown
particles. Pour contents of skillet into Crock-Pot over
chicken. Sprinkle with Italian seasoning. Cover and cook
on Low for 8 to 10 hours or on High for 3 to 4 hours).

Serve chicken over fluffy rice and spoon sauce over top.
Serves 4 to 6.

Each Serving:	Calories 477 kcal	Protein 42 gm
	Fat 31 gm	Carbohydrate 5 gm
	Sodium 257 mg	Cholesterol 173 mg

CHICKEN DELICIOUS

4-6 whole chicken breasts, boned and halved
lemon juice
salt and pepper
celery salt
paprika

1 can (10¾ ounces) condensed cream of mushroom soup

1 can (10¾ ounces) condensed cream of celery soup

⅓ cup dry sherry or white wine
grated Parmesan cheese
fluffy rice

Rinse chicken breasts and pat dry. Season with lemon juice, salt, pepper, celery salt and paprika. Place in Crock-Pot. In medium bowl or pan, mix mushroom and celery soups with sherry. Pour over chicken breasts. Sprinkle with Parmesan cheese. Cover and cook on Low for 8 to 10 hours or on High 4 to 5 hours.

Serve chicken and sauce over hot fluffy rice.
Serves 8 to 12.

Each Serving:	Calories 309 kcal	Protein 32 gm
	Fat 17 gm	Carbohydrate 5 gm
	Sodium 589 mg	Cholesterol 97 mg

HOT CHICKEN SALAD

2½ cups diced cooked chicken
1 cup toasted almonds
2 cups diagonally sliced celery
½ cup diced green pepper
3 tablespoons lemon juice
1 cup mayonnaise
3 tablespoons grated onion
1 cup cubed process cheese
1 cup crushed potato chips
½ cup grated Parmesan cheese
   toasted English muffins

Combine all ingredients in Crock-Pot except half the process cheese, half the potato chips, half the Parmesan cheese and the English muffins. Cover and cook on Low for 4 to 6 hours.

Just before serving, sprinkle with remaining process cheese, potato chips and Parmesan cheese. Serve on toasted English muffins. *Serves 6 to 8.*

Hot Turkey Salad: Substitute diced cooked turkey for the chicken.

Each Serving:	Calories 585 kcal	Protein 26 gm
	Fat 49 gm	Carbohydrate 12 gm
	Sodium 699 mg	Cholesterol 87 mg

COMPANY CHICKEN CASSEROLE

1   package (8 ounces) noodles
3   cups diced cooked chicken
$\frac{1}{2}$ cup diced celery
$\frac{1}{2}$ cup diced green pepper
$\frac{1}{2}$ cup diced onion
1   can (4 ounces) sliced mushrooms, drained
1   jar (4 ounces) pimiento, diced
$\frac{1}{2}$ cup grated Parmesan cheese
$1\frac{1}{2}$ cups cream-style cottage cheese
1   cup grated sharp process cheese
1   can ($10\frac{3}{4}$ ounces) condensed cream of chicken soup
$\frac{1}{2}$ cup chicken broth
2   tablespoons butter, melted
$\frac{1}{2}$ teaspoon leaf basil

Cook noodles according to package directions in boiling water until barely tender; drain and rinse thoroughly. In large bowl, combine remaining ingredients with noodles, making certain the noodles are separated and coated with liquid. Pour mixture into greased Crock-Pot. Cover and cook on Low for 6 to 10 hours or on High for 3 to 4 hours. *Serves 6.*

Company Turkey Casserole: Substitute diced cooked turkey for the chicken.

Each Serving:	Calories 532 kcal	Protein 41 gm
	Fat 24 gm	Carbohydrate 36 gm
	Sodium 1,253 mg	Cholesterol 144 mg

CHICKEN PIE

3 cups diced cooked chicken or turkey
2 cans (14½ ounces each) chicken broth
½ teaspoon salt
½ teaspoon black pepper
1 stalk celery, thinly sliced
1 medium onion, chopped
1 bay leaf
3 cups potatoes, peeled and cubed
1 package (16 ounces) frozen mixed vegetables
1 cup milk
1 cup all-purpose flour
1 teaspoon black pepper
½ teaspoon poultry seasoning
½ teaspoon salt
1 9-inch refrigerated pie crust

In Crock-Pot, combine meat, broth, ½ teaspoon salt, ½ teaspoon pepper, celery, onion, bay leaf, potatoes, and mixed vegetables. Cover; cook on Low 8 to 10 hours or on High 4 to 6 hours. Remove bay leaf.

Pre-heat oven to 400°. In a small bowl, mix milk and flour. Gradually stir flour mixture into the Crock-Pot. Stir in pepper, poultry seasoning, and salt. If using a removable Crock-Pot, carefully place 9-inch pie crust over vegetable-meat mixture. Place removable crock inside pre-heated oven, do not cover, bake for 15 minutes or until crust is browned. For a non-removable Crock-Pot, spoon vegetable-meat mixture into a 9 x 13 casserole dish. Roll out pie crust and carefully place on top of vegetable-meat mixture. Bake in oven for 15 minutes, until pie crust is brown. Serve immediately. *Serves 8.*

Each Serving:	Calories 677 kcal	Protein 47 gm
	Fat 12 gm	Carbohydrate 94 gm
	Sodium 634 mg	Cholesterol 49 mg

TURKEY OLE'

4 cups cooked turkey, shredded
1 package (1⅝ ounces) enchilada sauce mix
2 cans (6 ounces each) tomato paste
½ cup water
1 cup shredded Monterey Jack cheese
corns chips
Garnish: sour cream, sliced green onions, sliced ripe olives

Stir into Crock-Pot, shredded turkey meat, enchilada sauce mix, tomato paste, and water. Cover; cook on Low 7 to 8 hours or on High 3 to 4 hours. If on Low turn to High and add cheese. Allow cheese to melt. Serve with corn chips.

Variation: serve over cooked rice or noodles rather than with corn chips. Delicious also as a filling for tacos or tostadas.

Each Serving:	Calories 236 kcal	Protein 27 gm
	Fat 9 gm	Carbohydrate 14 gm
	Sodium 1,249 mg	Cholesterol 69 mg

SPICED TURKEY LOAF

With the emphasis on low fat meats, ground turkey is great to use in place of ground beef. This recipe brings a new blend of seasonings to the standard meat loaf.

2-2½ pounds ground turkey
1   medium onion, chopped
2   eggs
⅓   cup milk
2   tablespoons prepared horseradish
¼   cup bottled chili sauce
1   cup bread crumbs
1   teaspoon salt
2   cloves garlic minced, or ¼ teaspoon garlic powder
¼   cup chopped parsley
    sour cream for garnish

Mix all ingredients except garnish together. Form into loaf and lay atop meat rack or use foil handles (see page 219 for description of foil handles). Cook turkey loaf for 8 to 10 hours on Low or 5 to 6 hours on High. To ensure doneness insert meat thermometer in loaf. Thermometer should read 180°F. to indicate doneness. Serve with sour cream if desired. *Serves 8.*

Each Serving:	Calories 279 kcal	Protein 26 gm
	Fat 12 gm	Carbohydrate 15 gm
	Sodium 65 mg	Cholesterol 148 mg

TURKEY ENCHILADAS

Try this recipe for a fast easy dinner that will help you use up those Thanksgiving leftovers.

1   can (10 ounces) enchilada sauce
1   can (15½ ounces) dark red kidney beans
8   corn tortillas (6-inch)

1   cup shredded cooked turkey
1   cup shredded taco-flavored cheese

Place foil handles in Crock-Pot. Place 1 corn tortilla in bottom of Crock-Pot. Spoon small amount of enchilada sauce, beans, turkey and cheese over tortilla. Continue layering process until tortillas are gone. Make sure that last layer is the cheese layer. Cook on Low 6 to 8 hours or on High 3 to 4 hours. Pull out by foil handles and slice into pie shaped wedges for serving.

Each Serving:	Calories 199 kcal	Protein 12 gm
	Fat 6 gm	Carbohydrate 23 gm
	Sodium 694 mg	Cholesterol 27 mg

TURKEY AND TOMATO PASTA

A fast and healthy recipe. This meal is excellent for the weekend when you can just throw the ingredients in and come back later and dinner is ready.

1   can (14 ounces) whole tomatoes, chopped
1   can (28 ounces) whole tomatoes, chopped
2   teaspoons chili powder
1/2   teaspoon garlic powder
1   package (8 ounces) uncooked spiral pasta
1   cup cooked cubed turkey

Mix together tomatoes, chili powder, garlic powder, and turkey in Crock-Pot. Turn on High and let mixture heat through, approximately 1 to 1½ hours. Once mixture is heated, stir in uncooked pasta. Cook for an additional 30 minutes to 1 hour until pasta is tender.

Serves 4 (1 cup servings).

Each Serving:	Calories 334 kcal	Protein 21 gm
	Fat 3 gm	Carbohydrate 56 gm
	Sodium 525 mg	Cholesterol 27 mg

TURKEY MEATBALLS WITH GRAVY

2	beaten eggs
3/4	cup seasoned bread crumbs
1/2	cup chopped onion
1/2	cup finely chopped celery
2	tablespoons chopped parsley
1/2	teaspoon poultry seasoning
1/4	teaspoon black pepper
1/8	teaspoon garlic powder
2	pounds ground raw turkey
1-2	teaspoons vegetable oil
1	can (10³⁄4 ounces) undiluted cream of mushroom soup
1	cup water
1	envelope (1⁵⁄16 ounces) turkey gravy mix
1/2	teaspoon shredded lemon peel
1/4	teaspoon crushed dried thyme
1	bay leaf
	hot cooked mashed potatoes or buttered noodles

In a large bowl combine eggs, bread crumbs, onion, celery, parsley, poultry seasoning, pepper, and garlic. Add ground turkey and mix well. Shape into 1-inch balls.

In a large skillet brown meatballs in the cooking oil. Drain meatballs. Transfer to Crock-Pot. In a bowl combine soup water, gravy mix, lemon peel, thyme, and bay leaf. Pour over meatballs. Cover and cook on Low for 6 to 8 hours or on High for 3 to 4 hours. Discard bay leaf. Serve with mashed potatoes or buttered noodles. *Serves 8*.

Each Serving:	Calories 285 kcal	Protein 24 gm
	Fat 14 gm	Carbohydrate 14 gm
	Sodium 913 mg	Cholesterol 136 mg

SPICY TURKEY MEATBALLS

1   tablespoon olive oil or vegetable oil
1/4 cup minced onion
1   clove garlic, minced or 1/8 teaspoon garlic powder
1   pound ground turkey
1   cup plain bread crumbs
1   tablespoon rubbed sage
1   egg white
1   teaspoon grated orange peel
1/8 teaspoon cayenne pepper
1/4 teaspoon salt
    black pepper to taste
2   tablespoons chopped parsley
1   jar (16 ounces) spaghetti sauce

Combine onion, garlic, ground turkey, bread crumbs, sage, egg white, orange peel, cayenne, salt, black pepper, and parsley. Form into 1-inch balls and brown in skillet with 1 tablespoon oil. Drain meatballs and place in Crock-Pot. Cook on High 1 hour then stir in spaghetti sauce. Then cook on Low for 4 to 6 hours or on High for 2 to 3 hours. Serve over cooked spaghetti or cooked fettuccine. *Serves 6 to 8.*

Each Serving:	Calories 248 kcal	Protein 15 gm
	Fat 11 gm	Carbohydrate 23 gm
	Sodium 601 mg	Cholesterol 47 mg

CHEESY TURKEY COTTAGE FRIES

3-4	cups frozen cottage-style potatoes
1	cup pasteurized process cheese product
2	cups cubed, cooked turkey
1	jar (2 ounces) diced pimiento, drained
2	cups frozen cut broccoli, thawed and drained

Spray inside of Crock with cooking spray. Place potatoes in layer in bottom of Crock-Pot. Stir in remaining ingredients together and pour over potatoes. Cook on Low 6 to 8 hours or on High for 3 to 4 hours. *Serves 4 (1 cup servings).*

Each Serving:	Calories 397 kcal	Protein 31 gm
	Fat 16 gm	Carbohydrate 32 gm
	Sodium 617 mg	Cholesterol 80 mg

SWEET AND SOUR TURKEY

1	package (16 ounces) frozen broccoli, cauliflower, pea pods and yellow peppers, thawed and drained
1	cup cubed cooked turkey
2	bottles (11½ ounces each) sweet and sour sauce
1	can (11 ounces) Mandarin orange slices
1	can (8 ounces) pineapple chunks
3	cups uncooked converted white rice
2-3	cups water

In Crock-Pot combine vegetables, turkey, 1 bottle sweet and sour sauce, uncooked white rice, and water. Cook on

Low 6 to 8 hours or High 3 to 4 hours. In the last 30 minutes of cooking, stir in canned fruit and second bottle of sweet and sour sauce. *Serves 4.*

Each Serving:	Calories 838 kcal	Protein 62 gm
	Fat 4 gm	Carbohydrate 173 gm
	Sodium 464 mg	Cholesterol 29 mg

BREAKFAST CASSEROLE

This recipe can be prepared the night before in the removable Crock-Pot, refrigerated and then turned on in the morning for an excellent tasty brunch.

 2   tablespoons vegetable oil
 1   pound ground turkey sausage
 4   tablespoons chopped green onions
 6   cups cubed French bread
 2   cups shredded mild cheddar cheese, less fat
2⅔   cups skim milk
1¼   cup frozen egg substitute, thawed
 2   teaspoons prepared mustard
 ½   teaspoon ground black pepper

In a skillet brown turkey sausage and green onions in vegetable oil. Drain meat. Coat Crock-Pot with cooking spray and place bread cubes in bottom. Layer sausage mixture and cheese over bread. Combine milk, egg substitute, prepared mustard, and pepper. Pour over sausage and cheese. Cover and cook on High for 3 to 4 hours.

Prepared in a 4-quart Crock-Pot.

Each Serving:	Calories 218 kcal	Protein 19 gm
	Fat 10 gm	Carbohydrate 12 gm
	Sodium 567 mg	Cholesterol 43 mg

GROUND TURKEY TACOS

1	pound ground turkey
1	medium onion, chopped
1	can (4 ounces) sliced mushrooms, drained
1	garlic clove, minced or $1/8$ teaspoon garlic powder
1	can (6 ounces) tomato paste
$1/2$	cup white cooking wine
1	tablespoon chopped parsley
$1/2$	teaspoon salt
1	teaspoon pickling spices
4	whole peppercorns

Cream Sauce made with Yogurt:

1	tablespoon margarine or butter
1	tablespoon flour
$1/4$	teaspoon salt
$1/3$	cup milk
1	egg, slightly beaten
$1/2$	cup unflavored yogurt
	dash of ground nutmeg

Brown turkey and onion in skillet over medium heat. In Crock-Pot, combine turkey, onion, mushrooms, garlic, tomato paste, cooking wine, parsley, and salt. Tie pickling spices and peppercorns in a cheesecloth bag or tea ball. Add to the Crock-Pot; cover and cook on Low 4 to 5 hours. Remove spice bag. Prepare Cream Sauce as directed below. Spoon $1/4$ cup turkey mixture into each taco shell. Top with Cream Sauce. *Makes approximately 8 tacos.*

Cream Sauce:

In small saucepan, melt margarine or butter; stir in flour and salt. Gradually add milk, stirring continuously. Cook over low heat until thickened. Remove from heat. In small bowl, combine egg, yogurt, and nutmeg. Stir into hot mixture. Return to heat and cook over low heat for 1 minute, stirring continuously.

Each Serving:	Calories 150 kcal	Protein 13 gm
	Fat 7 gm	Carbohydrate 9 gm
	Sodium 586 mg	Cholesterol 71 mg

SOUPER RICE AND TURKEY

2   cans (10¾ ounces each) condensed cream of mushroom soup
3   cups water
3   cups uncooked converted white rice
1   cup thinly sliced celery
1   cup cubed cooked turkey
2   cups frozen peas and carrots or a frozen oriental vegetable mix
1   teaspoon poultry seasoning
1   tablespoon minced onion

Pour soup and water into Crock-Pot and mix. Add remaining ingredients and stir. Cook 6 to 8 hours on Low or 3 to 4 hours on High. Add soy sauce if desired.

Each Serving:	Calories 387 kcal	Protein 12 gm
	Fat 7 gm	Carbohydrate 67 gm
	Sodium 674 mg	Cholesterol 14 mg

TURKEY AND CORN CASSEROLE

Try this recipe to rid your refrigerator of those turkey leftovers.

1	tablespoon margarine or butter
1	onion, chopped
1	can (16 ounces) cream-style corn
4	large eggs
$1/2$	cup evaporated milk
$1/3$	cup all-purpose flour
	salt to taste
	black pepper to taste
2	cups cooked turkey, chopped
1	cup shredded cheddar cheese, sharp or mild

In a skillet melt the margarine over medium heat. Add the chopped onion and cook, stirring often until softened, about 5 minutes. Transfer to a medium-sized mixing bowl. Whisk the creamed corn, eggs, evaporated milk, flour, salt and pepper into the onion. Stir in the chopped turkey. Transfer to a lightly greased Crock-Pot.

Cover and cook on High for $2^1/2$ to 3 hours on High or until knife inserted comes out clean.

Sprinkle top of casserole with cheese; cover and cook until cheese is melted about 15 minutes. Serve immediately.

Each Serving:	Calories 297 kcal	Protein 23 gm
	Fat 14 gm	Carbohydrate 21 gm
	Sodium 390 mg	Cholesterol 175 mg

WILD GAME

BARBECUED VENISON

2-3 **pound venison round, leg or rump roast**
1 **can (12 ounces) beer**
3 **cloves garlic**
   salt and pepper
2 **onions, sliced**
3 **bay leaves**
2 **cups Barbecue Sauce (below)**

Trim excess fat from venison. In large bowl, mix beer, garlic, salt, pepper, onions and bay leaves; add venison. (Marinade should cover meat.) Marinate in refrigerator for 12 to 24 hours, turning occasionally. Remove venison and onions from marinade and place in Crock-Pot. Pour 1 cup Barbecue Sauce over top. Cover and cook on Low for 10 to 12 hours. Serve with remaining Barbecue Sauce. *Serves 6.*

Barbecue Sauce
1 **cup finely chopped onion**
3/4 **cup finely chopped celery**
3 **tablespoons butter**
6 **tablespoons sugar**
3 **tablespoons Worcestershire sauce**
6 **tablespoons wine vinegar**
3/4 **cup lemon juice**
3 **cups ketchup**
3 **teaspoons dry mustard**
2 **teaspoons liquid hickory smoke**
   salt and pepper

In skillet, sauté onion and celery in butter. Add to Crock-Pot with remaining ingredients. Cover and cook on Low for 8 to 10 hours or on High for 3 to 4 hours, stirring occasionally. *5 cups.*

Note: This sauce can be doubled, if desired; it freezes well, too.

Each Serving:	Calories 372 kcal	Protein 46 gm
	Fat 7 gm	Carbohydrate 29 gm
	Sodium 742 mg	Cholesterol 167 mg

RABBIT IN CREAM

1   large or 2 small rabbits, cut up
3   tablespoons minced ham or bacon
1   onion, finely chopped
½   teaspoon leaf thyme
1   can (4 ounces) sliced mushrooms, drained
1   cup beef bouillon
1   cup sour cream
2   tablespoons lemon juice
3   tablespoons flour
    minced parsley

Marinate rabbit overnight in refrigerator in salted water. Before cooking, remove rabbit pieces; drain and pat dry. Place rabbit, ham, onion, thyme and mushrooms in Crock-Pot. Pour in bouillon, moistening well. Cover and cook on Low for 8 to 10 hours.

Before serving, turn to High. Combine sour cream, lemon juice and flour. Remove rabbit to a warm platter. Stir sour cream mixture into Crock-Pot. Cook until thickened. Spoon sauce over rabbit and sprinkle with parsley. *Serves 6.*

Squirrel in Cream: Substitute 2 small squirrels, cut-up, for the rabbit.

Each Serving:	Calories 358 kcal	Protein 38 gm
	Fat 18 gm	Carbohydrate 8 gm
	Sodium 473 mg	Cholesterol 118 mg

BRAISED PHEASANT

2   pheasants (about 1½ pounds each) or
    1 pheasant (3 pounds), split
    salt and pepper
1   onion, sliced
2   carrots, pared and quartered
2   slices lean smoked bacon
¼   cup chicken broth
¼   cup dry sherry or broth

Season cavity of each pheasant lightly with salt and pepper. Arrange sliced vegetables in bottom of Crock-Pot. Place pheasants on top of vegetables. Cut bacon slices in half and place over each breast. Add broth and sherry. Cover and cook on Low for 8 to 10 hours or on High for 3 to 4 hours. *Serves 2 to 4.*

Each Serving:	Calories 780 kcal	Protein 92 gm
	Fat 38 gm	Carbohydrate 11 gm
	Sodium 313 mg	Cholesterol <1 mg

HASENPFEFFER

2½-3 pound rabbit, cut up
2   cups dry red wine
2   tablespoons wine vinegar
1   tablespoon sugar
1   tablespoon salt
1   teaspoon whole cloves
⅛   teaspoon pepper
2   bay leaves

Place cut-up rabbit in flat refrigerator container. In bowl, combine remaining ingredients; pour over rabbit. Marinate overnight in refrigerator. Place marinated rabbit in Crock-Pot. Add 1½ cups marinade. Cover and cook on Low for 8 to 10 hours.

Remove meat to warm platter. Thicken gravy, if desired. *Serves 4.*

Each Serving:	Calories 348 kcal	Protein 48 gm
	Fat 13 gm	Carbohydrate 6 gm
	Sodium 1,752 mg	Cholesterol 135 mg

VENISON STEW

2-3	pounds venison, cut into 1-inch cubes
1½	cups French dressing
2	carrots, pared and cut into 1- inch pieces
1	large onion, coarsely chopped
1	small green pepper, seeded and coarsely chopped
3	stalks celery, cut into 1-inch pieces
1	can (16 ounces) whole tomatoes, mashed
¼	cup quick-cooking tapioca
1	whole clove
1	bay leaf
	salt and pepper

Marinate cubed venison in French dressing for 12 to 24 hours in refrigerator. Drain off salad dressing and place venison in Crock-Pot. Stir in remaining ingredients. Cover and cook on Low for 8 to 10 hours. *Serves 6 to 8.*

Each Serving:	Calories 484 kcal	Protein 39 gm
	Fat 26 gm	Carbohydrate 23 gm
	Sodium 971 mg	Cholesterol 138 mg

QUAIL IN WINE-HERB SAUCE

12 quail
3 tablespoons flour
   salt and pepper
1 large onion, sliced
2 slices lean smoked bacon, diced
1 clove garlic, crushed
1 can (4 ounces) sliced mushrooms, drained
1 bay leaf
1/2 teaspoon leaf thyme
1/2 cup beef broth
1/2 cup dry white wine
   chopped parsley

Coat quail with a mixture of the flour, salt and pepper. Place onion slices in Crock-Pot; top with quail. Cover quail with diced bacon. Add remaining ingredients except parsley. Cover and cook on Low for 7 to 9 hours.

Remove quail to a heated platter and sprinkle with parsley. Thicken sauce, if desired, and spoon over quail. *Serves 6.*

Each Serving:	Calories 466 kcal	Protein 45 gm
	Fat 37 gm	Carbohydrate 8 gm
	Sodium 325 mg	Cholesterol <1 mg

FISH
AND
SEAFOOD

HALIBUT IN CREAMY WINE SAUCE

2	packages (12 ounces each) frozen halibut steaks, thawed
2	tablespoons flour
1	tablespoon sugar
1/4	teaspoon salt
1/4	cup butter
1/3	cup dry white wine
2/3	cup milk or half-and-half cream
	lemon wedges

Pat halibut steaks dry; place in Crock-Pot. Combine flour, sugar and salt.

In saucepan, melt butter; stir in flour mixture. When well blended, add wine and milk and cook over medium heat until thickened, stirring constantly. Allow sauce to boil 1 minute while stirring. Pour sauce over fish. Cover and cook on High 2 1/2 to 3 hours.

Transfer halibut to serving platter; garnish with lemon. *Serves 6.*

Each Serving:	Calories 212 kcal	Protein 20 gm
	Fat 11 gm	Carbohydrate 5 gm
	Sodium 232 mg	Cholesterol 54 mg

CLAM CASSEROLE

3	cans (6 1/2 ounces each) minced clams, drained
4	eggs, well beaten
1/4	cup butter, melted
1/3	cup milk
1	teaspoon salt

½   cup minced onion
¼   cup minced green pepper
18   saltine crackers, coarsely crushed (about 1 cup)

In bowl, mix all ingredients. Pour into well-greased Crock-Pot. Cover and cook on Low for 5 to 6 hours. *Serves 6.*

Each Serving:	Calories 242 kcal	Protein 18 gm
	Fat 14 gm	Carbohydrate 11 gm
	Sodium 665 mg	Cholesterol 196 mg

JAMBALAYA

2   cups diced boiled ham
2   medium onions, coarsely chopped
2   stalks celery, sliced
½   green pepper, seeded and diced
1   can (28 ounces) whole tomatoes
¼   cup tomato paste
3   cloves garlic, minced
1   tablespoon minced parsley
½   teaspoon leaf thyme
2   whole cloves
2   tablespoons salad oil
1   cup raw long-grain converted rice
1   pound fresh or frozen shrimp, shelled and cleaned

Thoroughly mix all ingredients except shrimp in Crock-Pot. Cover and cook on Low for 8 to 10 hours.

One hour before serving, turn Crock-Pot to High. Stir in uncooked shrimp. Cover and cook until shrimp are pink and tender. *Serves 4 to 6.*

Each Serving:	Calories 421 kcal	Protein 32 gm
	Fat 11 gm	Carbohydrate 49 gm
	Sodium 1,163 mg	Cholesterol 142 mg

CIOPPINO

1   pound sea bass, cut into chunks
1   can (4 ounces) sliced mushrooms, undrained
2   carrots, pared and sliced
1   medium onion, chopped
1   small green pepper, seeded and chopped
1   clove garlic, minced
1   can (15 ounces) tomato sauce
1   can (14 ounces) beef broth
    salt
1/8 teaspoon seasoned pepper
1/2 teaspoon leaf oregano
1   can (7 ounces) clams, undrained
1/2 pound shelled, cleaned shrimp
1   small lobster tail (optional)
1   package (6 ounces) frozen crabmeat, thawed
    and cartilage removed
    minced parsley

Combine half of sea bass in Crock-Pot with vegetables,
garlic, tomato sauce, beef broth and seasonings; stir well.
Cover and cook on Low for 10 to 12 hours or on High for
2 to 4 hours.

One hour before serving, turn to High and stir in
remaining sea bass and seafood. Cover and cook on
High for 1 hour or until done.

Garnish with minced parsley and serve in soup plates.
Accompany with hot Italian bread. *Serves 6.*

Each Serving:	Calories 223 kcal	Protein 34 gm
	Fat 3 gm	Carbohydrate 13 gm
	Sodium 1,182 mg	Cholesterol 128 mg

FISHERMAN'S CATCH CHOWDER

1-1½ pounds fish (use any combination of the
 following: flounder, ocean perch, pike,
 rainbow trout, haddock or halibut)
 ½ cup chopped onion
 ½ cup chopped celery
 ½ cup chopped pared carrots
 ¼ cup snipped parsley
 ¼ teaspoon leaf rosemary
 1 can (16 ounces) whole tomatoes, mashed
 ½ cup dry white wine
 1 bottle (8 ounces) clam juice
 1 teaspoon salt
 3 tablespoons flour
 3 tablespoons butter or margarine, melted
 ⅓ cup light cream

Cut cleaned fish into 1-inch pieces. Combine all
ingredients except flour, butter, and cream in Crock-Pot;
stir well. Cover and cook on Low for 7 to 8 hours or on
High for 3 to 4 hours.

One hour before serving, combine flour, butter and
cream. Stir into fish mixture. Continue to cook until
mixture is slightly thickened. *Serves 4.* Double recipe for
5-quart Crock-Pot.

Each Serving: Calories 308 kcal   Protein 30 gm
               Fat 15 gm   Carbohydrate 14 gm
               Sodium 1,096 mg   Cholesterol 104 mg

CHINESE CASHEW TUNA

1   can (7 ounces) tuna, drained and flaked
1   cup diced celery
$\frac{1}{2}$ cup minced onion
3   tablespoons margarine
1   can ($10\frac{3}{4}$ ounces) condensed cream of
     mushroom soup
1   can (16 ounces) bean sprouts, drained
1   tablespoon soy sauce
1   cup cashew nuts, coarsely chopped
1   can ($5\frac{1}{2}$ ounces) chow mein noodles

Combine all ingredients except chow mein noodles in
Crock-Pot; stir well. Cover and cook on Low for 5 to 9
hours or on High for 2 to 3 hours.

Serve over chow mein noodles. *Serves 4.*

Chinese Cashew Chicken: Substitute 1 cup diced
cooked chicken for the tuna.

Each Serving:	Calories 670 kcal	Protein 25 gm
	Fat 46 gm	Carbohydrate 44 gm
	Sodium 1,369 mg	Cholesterol 9 mg

TUNA SALAD CASSEROLE

2   cans (7 ounces each) tuna, drained and
     flaked
1   can ($10\frac{3}{4}$ ounces) condensed cream of celery
     soup
3   hard-cooked eggs, chopped
$1\frac{1}{2}$ cups diced celery
$\frac{1}{2}$ cup mayonnaise

¼   **teaspoon pepper**
1½   **cups crushed potato chips**

Combine all ingredients except ¼ cup of the crushed potato chips; stir well. Pour into greased Crock-Pot. Top with reserved potato chips. Cover and cook on Low for 5 to 8 hours. *Serves 4.*

Each Serving:	Calories 613 kcal	Protein 35 gm
	Fat 44 gm	Carbohydrate 19 gm
	Sodium 1,270 mg	Cholesterol 201 mg

SALMON AND POTATO CASSEROLE

4   **potatoes, peeled and thinly sliced**
3   **tablespoons flour**
    salt and pepper
1   **can (16 ounces) salmon, drained and flaked**
1   **medium onion, chopped**
1   **can (10¾ ounces) cream of mushroom soup**
¼   **cup water**
    nutmeg

Place half of the potatoes in greased Crock-Pot. Sprinkle with half of the flour, salt and pepper. Cover with half the salmon; sprinkle with half the onion. Repeat layers in order.

Combine soup and water. Pour over potato-salmon mixture. Dust with nutmeg. Cover and cook on Low for 7 to 10 hours. *Serves 6.*

Each Serving:	Calories 233 kcal	Protein 17 gm
	Fat 7 gm	Carbohydrate 25 gm
	Sodium 723 mg	Cholesterol 25 mg

SALMON-WICHES

1   can (16 ounces) salmon, drained and flaked
1   cup dry bread crumbs
2   eggs
¼   teaspoon leaf thyme
½   teaspoon celery salt
1   cup crushed cheese crackers
    vegetable oil
3   English muffins, split, toasted and buttered
2   cups Hollandaise sauce
    paprika

In bowl, combine salmon, bread crumbs, eggs, thyme and celery salt. Shape into 6 patties and coat well with crushed crackers. In skillet, sauté patties in hot oil; drain. Transfer to Crock-Pot. Cover and cook on High for 2 to 3 hours. Place one patty on each English muffin half and top with Hollandaise. Sprinkle with paprika. *Serves 6.*

Each Serving:	Calories 572 kcal	Protein 24 gm
	Fat 35 gm	Carbohydrate 41 gm
	Sodium 1,167 mg	Cholesterol 158 mg

SWEET-AND-SOUR SHRIMP

1 package (6 ounces) frozen Chinese pea pods, partially thawed
1 can (13 ounces) juice-pack pineapple chunks or tidbits (drain and reserve juice)
2 tablespoons cornstarch
3 tablespoons sugar
1 chicken bouillon cube
1 cup boiling water
1/2 cup reserved pineapple juice
2 teaspoons soy sauce
1/2 teaspoon ground ginger
2 cans (4 1/2 ounces each) shrimp, rinsed and drained
2 tablespoons cider vinegar
fluffy rice

Place pea pods and drained pineapple in Crock-Pot. In a small saucepan, stir together cornstarch and sugar. Dissolve bouillon cube in boiling water and add with juice, soy sauce and ginger to saucepan. Bring to a boil, stirring, and cook sauce for about 1 minute or until thickened and transparent. Gently blend sauce into pea pods and pineapple. Cover and cook on Low for 5 to 6 hours.

Before serving, add shrimp and vinegar, stirring carefully to avoid breaking up shrimp. Serve over hot rice. *Serves 4 to 5.*

Each Serving:	Calories 165 kcal	Protein 13 gm
	Fat 1 gm	Carbohydrate 26 gm
	Sodium 418 mg	Cholesterol 88 mg

EASY SHRIMP CREOLE

2	tablespoons butter or margarine
1/3	cup chopped onion
2	tablespoons buttermilk biscuit mix
1½	cups water
1	can (6 ounces) tomato paste
1	teaspoon salt
	dash pepper
¼	teaspoon sugar
1	bay leaf
½	cup chopped celery
½	cup chopped green pepper
2	pounds frozen shrimp, thawed, shelled and cleaned, or 3 cans (5 ounces each) shrimp, rinsed and drained
	fluffy rice

In skillet, melt butter; add onion and cook slightly. Add biscuit mix and stir until well blended. Combine remaining ingredients except shrimp and rice and add with onion mixture to Crock-Pot; stir well. Cover and cook on Low for 7 to 9 hours.

One hour before serving, turn to High and add shrimp. Remove bay leaf and serve over hot fluffy rice.

Serves 6. Double recipe for 5-quart Crock-Pot.

Each Serving:	Calories 206 kcal	Protein 26 gm
	Fat 7 gm	Carbohydrate 10 gm
	Sodium 849 mg	Cholesterol 197 mg

SWISS-CRAB CASSEROLE

3	tablespoons butter
1/2	cup chopped celery
1/2	cup chopped onion
1/4	cup chopped green pepper (optional)
3	tablespoons flour
3	chicken bouillon cubes
2 1/2	cups boiling water
1	cup quick-cooking rice
2	cans (7 ounces each) crabmeat, drained, flaked and cartilage removed
2	cups grated Swiss cheese
1	can (4 ounces) sliced mushrooms, drained
1/4	cup sliced pimiento-stuffed olives
1/4	cup sliced almonds (optional)
1	cup buttered bread crumbs
1/2	cup grated Swiss cheese

In skillet, melt butter and lightly sauté celery, onion and green pepper. Remove from heat and blend in flour. Dissolve bouillon cubes in boiling water. Add to skillet and bring to a boil, stirring constantly. Cook sauce over medium heat for about 2 minutes or until slightly thickened.

Lightly toss remaining ingredients except buttered crumbs and 1/2 cup grated cheese in Crock-Pot. Add sauce; stir lightly to blend. Cover and cook on High for 3 to 5 hours.

Pour contents of Crock-Pot into shallow heatproof serving dish. Cover with buttered bread crumbs and sprinkle with 1/2 cup grated cheese. Set under broiler until cheese is melted and bread crumbs are crunchy brown. *Serves 4 to 6.*

Each Serving:	Calories 545 kcal	Protein 34 gm
	Fat 27 gm	Carbohydrate 40 gm
	Sodium 1,427 mg	Cholesterol 129 mg

HERBED SALMON BAKE

2	chicken bouillon cubes
1	cup boiling water
1	can (16 ounces) salmon, drained and flaked
2	cups seasoned stuffing croutons
1	cup grated cheddar cheese
2	eggs, beaten
¼	teaspoon dry mustard

Dissolve bouillon cubes in boiling water. Combine all ingredients; mix well. Pour into well-greased Crock-Pot. Cover and cook on High for 2 to 4 hours. *Serves 4.*

Each Serving: Calories 443 kcal   Protein 34 gm
                        Fat 21 gm   Carbohydrate 28 gm
                        Sodium 1,652 mg   Cholesterol 173 mg

Soups, Stews, and Sauces

BEEF STOCK

- 3 beef soup bones
- 1-2 onions, chopped
- 1-2 carrots, pared and chopped
- 2 stalks celery, chopped
- 2 tablespoons dried parsley flakes
- 2 peppercorns
- 2 teaspoons salt

Place all ingredients in Crock-Pot. Add enough water to cover. Cover and cook on Low for 12 to 24 hours or on High for 4 to 6 hours. If cooked on High, the stock will be lighter in color and less concentrated. Strain and refrigerate. Keeps well 4 to 5 days, or may be frozen. *8 cups strained stock.*

Veal Stock: Substitute veal bones for the beef bones.

Each Serving:	Calories 27 kcal	Protein 5 gm
	Fat <1 gm	Carbohydrate 2 gm
	Sodium 625 mg	Cholesterol 0 mg

VEGETABLE CHEESE SOUP

- 1 can (16 ounces) cream-style corn
- 1 cup chopped, peeled potatoes
- 1 cup chopped carrots
- ½ cup chopped onion
- 1 teaspoon celery seed
- ½ teaspoon black pepper
- 2 cans (14½ ounces each) vegetable broth or chicken broth
- 1 jar (16 ounces) processed cheese

In Crock-Pot, combine corn, potatoes, carrots, onion, celery seed, and pepper. Add broth. Cover and cook on Low for 8 to 10 hours or on High 4 to 5 hours. If using

Low, turn to High. Stir cheese into Crock-Pot. Cover and cook 30 to 60 minutes or until cheese is melted and blended. Serve. *Serves 4 to 6.*

Time Saving Tip: A slight variation to the above recipe, that is also fast and easy to make. Omit the potatoes and chopped carrots. Stir in 1 10 oz. bag of frozen mixed vegetables. Cover and cook on High for 2-3 hours and then stir in cheese and continue to cook on High until well blended.

Each Serving:	Calories 386 kcal	Protein 18 gm
	Fat 21 gm	Carbohydrate 36 gm
	Sodium 2,288 mg	Cholesterol 50 mg

TWO-BEAN CORN CHILI

1   can (16 ounces) black-eyed peas
1   can (16 ounces) navy beans
1   onion, chopped
½   cup tomato paste
1   cup water
2   teaspoons chili powder
½   teaspoon ground cumin
¼   teaspoon dried oregano
1   teaspoon prepared mustard
1   cup fresh, frozen, or canned corn
½   cup chopped scallions
¼   cup diced canned jalapeño peppers
1   cup diced tomatoes

Combine above ingredients in Crock-Pot. Cover and cook on Low 8 to 10 hours or on High 4 to 5 hours. Serve. *Serves 6 to 8.*

Each Serving:	Calories 179 kcal	Protein 10 gm
	Fat 1 gm	Carbohydrate 34 gm
	Sodium 727 mg	Cholesterol <1 mg

CHICKEN AND RICE SOUP

1/2	cup sliced celery
1	pound boneless skinless chicken breasts, cooked and cut into pieces
3	cans (14 1/2 ounces each) chicken broth
1/2	cup water
2	cups frozen mixed vegetables
3/4	cup uncooked converted white rice
1	tablespoon parsley flakes
2	teaspoons lemon and herb seasoning

Combine above ingredients in Crock-Pot. Cover and cook on Low 6 to 8 hours or on High for 3 to 4 hours. Serve.

If cooking on High, place celery in dish in microwave with a tablespoon of water and cover. Microwave until celery is slightly soft, then add to Crock-Pot and cook on High.

If soup is a little too thick, add more water for a thinner soup. Allow to cook 15 minutes. *Serves 4 to 6.*

Each Serving:	Calories 284 kcal	Protein 28 gm
	Fat 4 gm	Carbohydrate 33 gm
	Sodium 1,324 mg	Cholesterol 53 mg

REUBEN SOUP

An old world favorite, sauerkraut takes on a new meaning in this soup. It is sure to be a hit with Reuben sandwich connoisseurs.

1	cup chopped onion
1	cup celery
1/4	cup margarine or butter
2	cups chicken broth
2	cups beef broth
1	teaspoon baking soda
1/4	cup cornstarch
1/4	cup water
1 1/2	cups sauerkraut, rinsed and drained
4	cups milk
4	cups chopped, cooked corned beef

2 cups shredded Swiss cheese
salt
black pepper
Rye croutons, optional

Chop onion and celery. Transfer to Crock-Pot. Stir in broth and baking soda. Combine corn starch and water and add to Crock-Pot. Stir in sauerkraut, milk, and corned beef. Cover and cook on High 4 to 5 hours. Stir in cheese and cook 30 minutes. Season with salt and pepper. Serve. Garnish with croutons if desired. *Serves 12.*

Each Serving:	Calories 301 kcal	Protein 18 gm
	Fat 21 gm	Carbohydrate 9 gm
	Sodium 1,286 mg	Cholesterol 75 mg

BLACK BEAN AND POTATO SOUP

1 can (16 ounces) black beans, drained
2 potatoes, washed and diced
½ pound cooked ham, cut in pieces
6 cups beef broth
¼ cup dried chopped onions
1 4-ounce can chopped jalapeño peppers or mild chili peppers
1 clove garlic, minced
1 teaspoon ground cumin
1 teaspoon ground oregano
1 teaspoon ground thyme
⅛ teaspoon ground cloves
Garnish: sour cream and chopped tomatoes

In Crock-Pot, combine beans, potatoes, ham, broth, onion, peppers, garlic, cumin, oregano, thyme, and cloves. Cover and cook on Low 8 to 10 hours or on High 4 to 5 hours. Serve. Garnish bowls with sour cream and chopped tomatoes if desired. *Serves 6 to 8*

Each Serving:	Calories 186 kcal	Protein 14 gm
	Fat 4 gm	Carbohydrate 23 gm
	Sodium 2,382 mg	Cholesterol 19 mg

BEEF STEW

2	pounds beef stew meat
1/2	cup all-purpose flour
3	tablespoons shortening
1	medium onion, chopped
4	carrots, sliced
3	celery stalks, sliced
1	clove garlic, minced
2	bay leaves
1	teaspoon salt
1	teaspoon sugar
1/2	teaspoon black pepper
1/2	teaspoon paprika
1/8	teaspoon ground cloves
1	teaspoon lemon juice
1	teaspoon Worcestershire sauce
4	cups water

Dredge meat in flour, melt shortening in skillet. Add beef cubes to skillet and sauté until evenly browned. Transfer to Crock-Pot. Add onion, carrots, celery, garlic, and other seasonings. Pour in water and stir. Cover and cook on Low 10 to 12 hours or on High 5 to 6 hours. Serve. *Serves 8 to 10.*

Each Serving:	Calories 347 kcal	Protein 19 gm
	Fat 25 gm	Carbohydrate 12 gm
	Sodium 342 mg	Cholesterol 73 mg

ONION AND CHEESE SOUP

$1/4$ cup margarine or butter
  2   large red onions, thinly sliced
  2   large yellow onions, thinly sliced
$1/2$ teaspoon salt
$1/2$ teaspoon black pepper
$1/4$ cup white cooking wine
$2^2/3$ cups beef broth
  2   cups water
$1/4$ teaspoon dried thyme
  8   slices French bread
      olive oil or vegetable oil
  3   cups shredded Swiss cheese

In a skillet, melt the margarine over medium heat. Add the red and yellow onions. Sauté the onions until tender. Stir in the sugar, salt, and pepper. Cook 20 minutes, stirring occasionally. Transfer to Crock-Pot. Stir in the cooking wine, broth, water, and thyme. Cover and cook on Low 6 to 8 hours or on High 3 to 4 hours.

Before serving, preheat oven to 400°. Place the bread slices on a baking sheet and brush with oil. Bake 10 to 15 minutes or until toasted. Place half the bread slices in a large serving bowl and sprinkle with half the cheese; repeat the layering process. Pour the hot soup into the serving bowl. Cover and let stand for 5 minutes. Serve. *Serves 6 to 8.*

Each Serving:	Calories 413 kcal	Protein 19 gm
	Fat 25 gm	Carbohydrate 28 gm
	Sodium 1,220 mg	Cholesterol 45 mg

BEAN, HAM AND PASTA SOUP

This hearty soup makes a great main dish when served with a side of your choice of bread.

- **1 cup dried pinto beans, rinsed, drained and picked over**
- **2 tablespoons olive oil**
- **1/2 pound smoked ham, chopped**
- **1 medium onion, finely chopped**
- **1 medium celery rib, finely chopped**
- **2 garlic cloves, minced**
- **2 2/3 cups double strength chicken broth, canned or homemade**
- **3 cups water**
- **1/4 cup tomato paste**
- **1/2 cup spaghetti broken into 1-inch pieces, or bow-tie pasta or shells**
- **1/4 teaspoon salt**
- **1/4 teaspoon black pepper**

In a large bowl, combine the beans and enough water to cover by 2 inches. Let stand overnight; drain well.

In a large skillet, heat the oil over medium-high heat. Add the ham, onion, and celery and cook, stirring often until lightly browned, about 6 minutes. Add the garlic and cook, stirring often, for 1 minute. Add the chicken broth, stirring to scrape up the browned bits on the bottom of the skillet. Transfer to a 3 1/2-quart slow cooker.

Add the drained beans, water, and tomato paste. Cover and slow cook until the beans are tender, 7 to 8 hours on Low or 4 to 5 hours on High.

Stir in the pasta, salt, and pepper. Turn heat to high and cook until the pasta is tender, about 30 to 60 minutes.

Using a large spoon, crush enough of the beans against the sides of the slow cooker to reach the consistency you like. Serve immediately. *Serves 6 to 8.*

Each Serving:	Calories 250 kcal	Protein 18 gm
	Fat 7 gm	Carbohydrate 29 gm
	Sodium 1,223 mg	Cholesterol 16 mg

FIVE-ALARM BEEF CHILI

Try this chili as is or increase the seasonings or peppers as you would like to increase the chili flavor or the heat.

1/4 cup vegetable oil or olive oil
3-4 pounds boneless beef chuck, cut into pieces
2 onions, chopped
2 green bell peppers, chopped
1 can (4 ounces) chopped jalapeños or mild chili peppers
1/3 cup chili powder
1 tablespoon dried oregano
2 teaspoons ground cumin
1 teaspoon salt
1 cup beer

Heat 2 tablespoons of oil in a skillet over medium heat. Add the beef and brown all sides. Transfer to Crock-Pot. Add the remaining 2 tablespoons oil to the skillet and sauté the onions and green peppers until soft. Transfer to Crock-Pot. In Crock-Pot, stir in the jalapeños, chili powder, oregano, cumin, salt, and beer. Cover and cook on Low 6 to 8 hours or on High 3 to 4 hours. Serve. *Serves 6 to 8.*

Each Serving:	Calories 701 kcal	Protein 41 gm
	Fat 55 gm	Carbohydrate 11 gm
	Sodium 765 mg	Cholesterol 163 mg

NO BEANS BEEF CHILI WITH CORNMEAL

Try this mild tasting chili with cornmeal for a hearty meal that should be enjoyed by all.

- 2 **pounds ground beef**
- 1 **onion, chopped**
- 1 **green pepper**
- 2 **cloves garlic, minced**
- 1 **can (10 ounces) enchilada sauce**
- 1 **can (8 ounces) tomato sauce**
- 1 **can (4½ ounces) chopped black olives, drained**
- 2 **tablespoons chili powder**
- 1 **teaspoon salt**
- 1 **teaspoon dried oregano**
- ½ **teaspoon ground cumin**
- 2 **cups water**
- 1 **cup yellow cornmeal**
- 2 **cups shredded cheddar cheese**

In a skillet over medium heat, cook the ground beef, onion, and green pepper until the meat turns brown. Drain fat. Transfer to Crock-Pot. Stir in enchilada sauce, tomato sauce, olives, chili powder, salt, oregano, and cumin. Cover and cook on Low for 8 to 10 hours or on High for 4 to 5 hours.

In a saucepan, bring the 2 cups of water to a boil and gradually stir in the cornmeal. Reduce heat to low and cook until thick. Drop the cornmeal by tablespoons onto the chili. Increase heat to high if cooking on low. Cover and cook 20 to 25 minutes. Sprinkle cornmeal with cheese and cook until cheese is melted. Serve. *Serves 6 to 8*

Each Serving:	Calories 573 kcal	Protein 33 gm
	Fat 37 gm	Carbohydrate 28 gm
	Sodium 1,360 mg	Cholesterol 120 mg

WHITE CHILI

This flavorful version of "White Chili" will surprise even the most discernible taste buds.

- 1 can (16 ounces) navy beans, drained
- 4 cans (14½ ounces each) chicken broth
- 1 onion, chopped
- 2 cloves garlic, minced
- 1 tablespoon ground white pepper
- 1 tablespoon dried oregano
- 1 tablespoon ground cumin
- 1 teaspoon salt
- ¼ teaspoon ground cloves
- 5 cups chopped cooked chicken
- 2 cans (4 ounces each) chopped green chiles
- 1 cup water
- 8 flour tortillas
  Monterey Jack cheese
  salsa
  sour cream

In Crock-Pot, combine beans, broth, onion, garlic, white pepper, oregano, cumin, salt, cloves, chicken, green chiles, and water. Cover and cook on Low 8 to 10 hours or on High 4 to 5 hours.

To serve, make 4 cuts in each tortilla toward center, but not through and line serving bowls with tortillas, overlapping edges. Spoon in chili. Top with cheese, salsa, and sour cream. Serve immediately. *Serves 8.*

Each Serving:	Calories 394 kcal	Protein 35 gm
	Fat 11 gm	Carbohydrate 36 gm
	Sodium 1,822 mg	Cholesterol 78 mg

CHICKEN TORTILLA SOUP

$1^1/_2$ pounds boneless chicken, cooked and shredded
  1   can (15 ounces) whole tomatoes
  1   can (10 ounces) enchilada sauce
  1   medium onion, chopped
  1   can (4 ounces) chopped green chilies
  1   clove garlic, minced
  2   cups water
  1   can ($14^1/_2$ ounces) chicken broth
  1   teaspoon cumin
  1   teaspoon chili powder
  1   teaspoon salt
$^1/_4$ teaspoon black pepper
  1   bay leaf
  1   package (10 ounces) frozen corn
  1   tablespoon dried chopped cilantro
  6   corn tortillas
  2   tablespoons vegetable oil
      grated Parmesan cheese for garnish

In Crock-Pot, combine the shredded chicken, whole tomatoes, enchilada sauce, onion, green chilies, and garlic. Add the water, chicken broth, cumin, chili powder, salt, black pepper, and bay leaf. Stir in the corn and cilantro. Cover and cook on Low 6 to 8 hours or on High 3 to 4 hours.

Preheat oven to 400°. Lightly brush both sides of tortillas with vegetable oil. Cut the tortillas into strips that are $2^1/_2$ -inches long and $^1/_2$ inch wide. Spread the tortilla strips onto a baking sheet. Bake, turning occasionally, until crisp, 5 to 10 minutes. Sprinkle tortilla strips and grated Parmesan cheese over soup. Serve. *Serves 6 to 8.*

Each Serving:	Calories 286 kcal	Protein 25 gm
	Fat 9 gm	Carbohydrate 29 gm
	Sodium 1,267 mg	Cholesterol 68 mg

VEGETABLE AND PASTA SOUP

1	onion, chopped
2	carrots, peeled and thinly sliced
2	zucchini, thinly sliced
1	can (14 ounces) whole tomatoes
2	cans (14½ ounces each) beef broth
1½	cups water
1	tablespoon plus 4 teaspoons dried parsley flakes
1	tablespoon oregano
1½	cups small shell-shaped pasta, uncooked Grated Parmesan cheese

In Crock-Pot, combine onion, carrots, zucchini, tomatoes, broth, water, parsley, and oregano. Cover and cook on Low 8 to 10 hours or High for 4 to 5 hours. Stir in uncooked pasta and cook for an additional 30 minutes or until pasta is tender. Garnish with grated Parmesan cheese. Serve. *Serves 6 to 8.*

Each Serving:	Calories 121 kcal	Protein 5 gm
	Fat <1 gm	Carbohydrate 23 gm
	Sodium 924 mg	Cholesterol <1 mg

VEGETABLE CHILI

Not only is this chili meatless, but colorful as well with a medley of fresh vegetables.

1   can (16 ounces) garbanzo beans, drained
1   large onion, chopped
1   can (4 ounces) chopped green chiles
2   cloves garlic, minced
1/3 cup chili powder
1   tablespoon dried oregano
2   teaspoons ground cumin
1   can (28 ounces) whole tomatoes, undrained
2   carrots, thinly sliced
2   celery ribs, thinly sliced
2   zucchini, thinly sliced
1   red bell pepper, seeded and chopped
1   green bell pepper, seeded and chopped
1   teaspoon salt
    sour cream for garnish

In Crock-Pot, combine the beans, onion, green chiles, garlic, chili powder, oregano, cumin, tomatoes, carrots, celery, zucchini, red and green bell pepper, and salt. Cover and cook on Low 6 to 8 hours or High 3 to 4 hours. Cook until vegetables are tender. Serve immediately. Garnish with sour cream if desired. *Serves 6 to 8.*

Each Serving:	Calories 162 kcal	Protein 7 gm
	Fat 2 gm	Carbohydrate 33 gm
	Sodium 870 mg	Cholesterol <1 mg

THREE BEAN-
TURKEY SOUP

1 pound ground turkey
1 cup chopped onion
¾ green pepper
2 cloves garlic, minced
1 can (16 ounces) red kidney beans, drained
1 can (16 ounces) Great Northern Beans or
   Pinto beans, drained
1 can (16 ounces) black beans
3 cups water
2 cans (14½ ounces) whole tomatoes,
   undrained and chopped
1 can (8 ounces) tomato sauce
2 cups sliced carrots
2 teaspoons dried oregano
½ teaspoon dried thyme
½ teaspoon chicken-flavored bouillon granules
½ teaspoon salt
½ teaspoon black pepper

In a skillet, brown turkey, onions, green pepper, and
garlic. Drain fat. Transfer to Crock-Pot. Add beans,
water, tomatoes, sauce, carrots, and seasonings. Stir.
Cover and cook on Low 8 to 10 hours or on High 4 to 5
hours. Before serving, mash beans slightly for a thicker
soup if desired. Serve. *Serves 10 to 12.*

Each Serving:	Calories 212 kcal	Protein 16 gm
	Fat 4 gm	Carbohydrate 29 gm
	Sodium 651 mg	Cholesterol 30 gm

SPICY CABBAGE-BEEF SOUP

*Here's a flavorful soup that is sure to be a crowd pleaser.
Leftovers? Just freeze and reheat at a later date.*

1	pound ground beef
1	large onion, chopped
5	cups chopped cabbage (bite-size pieces)
2	cans (16 ounces each) red kidney beans
3	cans (8 ounces each) tomato sauce
2	cups water
1	green bell pepper, chopped
3/4	cup picante sauce
4	beef bouillon cubes
1 1/2	teaspoon ground cumin
1/2	teaspoon salt
1/4	teaspoon black pepper

Brown ground beef and onion over medium heat in a skillet.
Drain. Pour into Crock-Pot. Stir in cabbage, beans, tomato
sauce, water, pepper, picante sauce, beef bouillon, and
seasonings. Cover and cook on Low 6 to 8 hours or High
3 to 4 hours. Serve when cabbage is tender. *Serves 10 to 12.*

Each Serving:	Calories 208 kcal	Protein 13 gm
	Fat 8 gm	Carbohydrate 22 gm
	Sodium 1,211 mg	Cholesterol 28 mg

CREAMY VEGETABLE SOUP

1	large onion, chopped
1/4	cup margarine or butter, melted
3	medium sweet potatoes, peeled and chopped
3	zucchini, chopped

1-2 cups chopped broccoli
3 cans (14$\frac{1}{2}$ ounces each) chicken broth
2 medium potatoes, peeled and shredded
$\frac{1}{2}$ teaspoon celery seed
2 teaspoons salt
1 teaspoon ground cumin
1 teaspoon black pepper
2 cups milk

In Crock-Pot, stir together, onion, margarine, sweet potatoes, zucchini, and broccoli. Pour in chicken broth and stir. Add potatoes, and seasonings. Stir. Cover and cook on Low 8 to 10 hours or on High 4 to 5 hours. Add milk and cook 30 minutes to 1 hour. Serve. *Serves 12.*

Each Serving:	Calories 151 kcal	Protein 5 gm
	Fat 6 gm	Carbohydrate 20 gm
	Sodium 881 mg	Cholesterol 6 mg

OLD-FASHIONED ONION SOUP

3 pounds large onions, peeled and thinly sliced
$\frac{1}{2}$ cup butter, melted
6-8 slices French bread, cubed
4-5 cups chicken broth

Place sliced onions in Crock-Pot; pour in butter and mix to coat onions thoroughly. Stir in cubed bread. Add chicken broth to cover; stir well. Cover and cook on Low for 10 to 18 hours or on High for 4 to 5 hours, stirring occasionally. Stir well during last hour. *Serves 6 to 8.*

Each Serving:	Calories 271 kcal	Protein 6 gm
	Fat 15 gm	Carbohydrate 28 gm
	Sodium 934 mg	Cholesterol 36 mg

GERMAN POTATO SOUP

This flavorful soup makes a hearty main dish for those cold winter nights with a loaf of French bread.

1	pound bacon, cooked and diced
1	onion, chopped
1	leek, trimmed and diced
2	carrots, peeled and diced
1	cup chopped cabbage
1/4	cup chopped parsley
4	cups beef broth
1	pound potatoes, washed and diced
1	bay leaf
2	teaspoons black pepper
1	teaspoon salt
1/2	teaspoon caraway seeds
1/4	teaspoon nutmeg
1/2	cup sour cream

Combine onion, leek, carrots, cabbage, parsley, broth, and potatoes to Crock-Pot. Stir in seasonings. Cover and cook on Low 8 to 10 hours or High 4 to 5 hours. Remove bay leaf. Using a slotted spoon remove potatoes and mash. Combine potatoes with sour cream. Return to Crock-Pot and stir. Stir in bacon pieces. Serve. *Serves 6 to 8.*

For the 6-quart, use 6 cups of beef broth, 2 leeks, 3 carrots, diced, and 2 pounds of potatoes. Season as desired.

Each Serving:	Calories 236 kcal	Protein 9 gm
	Fat 13 gm	Carbohydrate 20 gm
	Sodium 1,568 mg	Cholesterol 23 mg

PORK, POTATO, AND GREEN BEAN STEW

This stew's combination of ingredients is sure to be a mealtime favorite.

- 2 cans (14½ ounces each) chicken broth
- 1 pound boneless pork loin, trimmed of fat, and cut into pieces
- 4 red potatoes, cut into ½-inch cubes
- 1 onion, chopped
- 2 garlic cloves, minced
- ⅓ cup all-purpose flour
- 2 cups frozen cut green beans
- 2 teaspoons Worcestershire sauce
- ½ teaspoon dried thyme leaves
- ½ teaspoon black pepper

Heat pork loin, potatoes, onion, and garlic with 1 can chicken broth in skillet for 5 to 10 minutes over medium heat. Transfer to Crock-Pot.

Combine ¾ cup chicken broth and flour in a small bowl. Set aside.

Add remaining broth, green beans, Worcestershire sauce, thyme, and pepper to Crock-Pot and stir. Cover and cook 8 to 10 hours on Low or 4 to 5 hours on High. If on Low, turn to High and stir in flour mixture. Cook 30 minutes to thicken. Serve. *Serves 8.*

Each Serving:	Calories 203 kcal	Protein 16 gm
	Fat 5 gm	Carbohydrate 24 gm
	Sodium 489 mg	Cholesterol 34 mg

CHICKEN AND SAUSAGE GUMBO

3/4	cup all-purpose flour
1/2	pound smoked sausage, sliced
3/4	pound chicken breasts, cooked and shredded
1	cup chopped onion
1/2	cup chopped green pepper
1/2	cup chopped celery
8	cups water
2	cloves garlic, minced
1	bay leaf
1 1/2	teaspoon Cajun seasoning
1	teaspoon salt
1/2	teaspoon dried thyme
1/4	teaspoon black pepper
1	tablespoon Worcestershire sauce
	dash hot sauce
3/4	cup sliced green onions
4	cups hot cooked rice

Prepare chicken breasts and shred. Set aside. Brown sausage, onion, and green pepper in skillet. Drain fat. In Crock-Pot, combine shredded chicken, sausage mixture, celery, water, and seasonings. Cover and cook on Low 6 to 8 hours or on High 3 to 4 hours. Serve over rice and garnish with the green onions. *Serves 8 to 10.*

Each Serving:	Calories 317 kcal	Protein 18 gm
	Fat 9 gm	Carbohydrate 38 gm
	Sodium 813 mg	Cholesterol 41 mg

MEATBALL STEW

1	pound lean ground beef
1	medium onion, chopped
1	egg
1	cup dry bread crumbs
$1/2$	teaspoon salt
$1/4$	teaspoon pepper
2	tablespoons margarine or butter
1	can (16 ounces) whole tomatoes, undrained, chopped
1	cup water
2	tablespoons beef flavor base (paste or granules)
$1/4$	teaspoon garlic powder
$1/2$	teaspoon seasoned salt
2	teaspoons Italian seasoning
4	carrots, pared and sliced
3	large potatoes, peeled and diced
1	medium onion, sliced
2	tablespoons cornstarch
$1/4$	cup cold water

Combine ground beef with chopped onion, egg, bread crumbs, salt and pepper. Shape mixture into about 24 meatballs, then brown in margarine; drain well.

Stir together tomatoes, water, beef base and seasonings. Place carrots, potatoes and sliced onion in bottom of Crock-Pot; top with meatballs. Pour tomato mixture over all. Cover and cook on Low for 8 to 10 hours.

Before serving, remove meatballs with a slotted spoon. Make a smooth paste of the cornstarch and water and stir into vegetables. Cover and cook on High for 10 minutes to thicken. Return meatballs to stew and serve. *Serves 6.*

Each Serving:	Calories 461 kcal	Protein 21 gm
	Fat 22 gm	Carbohydrate 45 gm
	Sodium 1,542 mg	Cholesterol 92 mg

MINESTRONE SOUP

2 packages (16 ounces each) frozen vegetables and pasta in garlic seasoned sauce
4 cups reduced-sodium vegetable juice cocktail
2 cans (15½ ounces each) red kidney beans, drained and rinsed
1 cup beef broth
1 tablespoon minced onion
½ teaspoon dried Italian seasoning
½ teaspoon dried basil
½ teaspoon salt
½ teaspoon black pepper

Combine all ingredients in Crock-Pot. Cover and cook on Low 4 to 6 hours or High for 2 to 3 hours. Serve. *Serves 8.*

Each Serving:	Calories 265 kcal	Protein 11 gm
	Fat 8 gm	Carbohydrate 40 gm
	Sodium 1,025 mg	Cholesterol 9 mg

 # SAUSAGE-BEAN SOUP

1 pound bulk Italian sausage or Kielbasa cut into pieces
½ cup chopped onion
2 cloves garlic, minced
1 teaspoon dried basil leaves
1 can (16 ounces) whole tomatoes, undrained, cut up
1 can (14½ ounces) beef broth
1 can (15 ounces) black beans, undrained
1 can (15 ounces) butter beans, undrained
grated Parmesan cheese for garnish

In a skillet, brown sausage, onion, and garlic. Drain fat.

Transfer to Crock-Pot. Stir in remaining ingredients except for the Parmesan cheese. Cover and cook on Low 6 to 8 hours or on High 3 to 4 hours. Ladle into bowls and top serving with Parmesan cheese if desired. *Serves 6.*

Each Serving:	Calories 362 kcal	Protein 23 gm
	Fat 18 gm	Carbohydrate 30 gm
	Sodium 1,713 mg	Cholesterol 51 mg

MINESTRONE HAMBURGER SOUP

1   pounds lean ground beef
1   large onion, chopped
2   small potatoes, peeled and cubed
2   carrots, pared and sliced
2   stalks celery, sliced
1   can (28 ounces) whole tomatoes
1   cup shredded cabbage
1   small bay leaf
1/4   teaspoon leaf thyme
1/4   teaspoon leaf basil
1   teaspoon salt
1/4   teaspoon pepper
     grated mozzarella or Parmesan cheese

Place all ingredients except cheese in Crock-Pot; stir thoroughly. Add water to cover. Cover and cook on Low for 8 to 12 hours or on High for 3 to 5 hours. Stir well. Serve sprinkled with cheese. *Serves 6.*

Each Serving:	Calories 287 kcal	Protein 16 gm
	Fat 16 gm	Carbohydrate 20 gm
	Sodium 660 mg	Cholesterol 57 mg

VEGETABLE BEEF

3-4	pound beef round or chuck steak, $1^1/2$-inches thick, cut into $1^1/2$-inch cubes
$^1/3$	cup flour
1	teaspoon salt
$^1/2$	teaspoon cracked pepper
2-3	carrots, pared, split lengthwise and cut in half
2	large stalks celery, cut into 1-inch pieces
6	small white onions
6-8	small new potatoes, peeled
1	can (4 ounces) sliced mushrooms, drained
1	package (10 ounces) frozen peas, corn, green beans or lima beans, partially thawed
1	can ($10^1/2$ ounces) condensed beef broth
$^1/2$	cup dry red wine or water
2	teaspoons brown sugar
2	teaspoons Kitchen Bouquet
1	can ($14^1/2$ ounces) tomato wedges or slices, drained (optional)
$^1/4$	cup flour
$^1/4$	cup water

If beef is extra lean, thoroughly wipe cubed beef on absorbent towels to dry. If meat contains fat, quickly brown in large skillet to sear and remove fat; drain well.

Place beef cubes in Crock-Pot. Combine $^1/3$ cup flour with the salt and pepper; toss with beef to coat thoroughly. Add all vegetables except tomato wedges to Crock-Pot and mix well. Combine beef broth, wine, sugar and kitchen bouquet. Pour over meat and vegetables; stir carefully. Add drained tomatoes and stir well. Cover and cook on Low for 10 to 14 hours or on High for 4 to $5^1/2$ hours.

One hour before serving, turn to High. Make a smooth paste of ¼ cup flour and the water; stir into Crock-Pot. Cover and cook until thickened. *Serves 8 to 10.*

Note: For better color, add half of the frozen vegetables at beginning; add remaining half during last hour.

Each Serving:	Calories 354 kcal	Protein 44 gm
	Fat 9 gm	Carbohydrate 23 gm
	Sodium 669 mg	Cholesterol 102 mg

HUNGARIAN BEEF STEW

2 pounds lean stewing beef, cut into 1½-inch cubes
1 large onion, finely chopped
2 medium potatoes, peeled and cubed
2 carrots, pared and sliced
1 package (10 ounces) frozen lima beans, thawed
2 cloves garlic, chopped
1 green pepper, seeded and cut into strips
2 teaspoons dried parsley flakes
½ cup beef broth
2 teaspoons paprika
1 teaspoon salt
1 can (16 ounces) whole tomatoes

Place all ingredients except beef broth, paprika, salt and tomatoes in Crock-Pot. Mix beef broth, paprika, salt and tomatoes; pour over top and stir to blend. Cover and cook on Low for 10 to 12 hours or on High for 5 to 6 hours. *Serves 4 to 6.*

Each Serving:	Calories 429 kcal	Protein 42 gm
	Fat 14 gm	Carbohydrate 33 gm
	Sodium 940 mg	Cholesterol 118 mg

BACHELOR'S STEW

2 pounds beef chuck, cut into 1- to 2-inch cubes
⅓ cup dry bread crumbs
1 teaspoon salt
⅛ teaspoon pepper
1 large onion, cut into eighths
3 carrots, pared, split lengthwise and cut into 4-inch strips
4 celery stalks, cut into 1-inch pieces
1 teaspoon leaf basil
⅓ cup quick-cooking tapioca
1 can (4 ounces) sliced mushrooms, undrained
1 teaspoon Kitchen Bouquet
2 cans (10¾ ounces each) condensed tomato soup
1 cup beef broth or water

Wipe beef cubes well. Combine bread crumbs with salt and pepper and toss with beef. Place coated beef cubes in Crock-Pot and add remaining ingredients; stir well. Cover and cook on Low for 10 to 12 hours or on High for 3 to 5 hours. *Serves 6.*

Each Serving:	Calories 552 kcal	Protein 30 gm
	Fat 33 gm	Carbohydrate 35 gm
	Sodium 1,653 mg	Cholesterol 109 mg

 # *GOOD 'N EASY STEW*

3 pounds lean stewing beef, cut into 1½-inch cubes
1 envelope (1½ ounces) dry onion soup mix
½ cup sauterne wine or beef broth

1   can (10½ ounces) condensed cream of
    mushroom soup or cream of celery soup
1   can (4 ounces) sliced mushrooms, drained
    (optional)

Combine all ingredients in Crock-Pot. Cover and cook on
Low for 10 to 12 hours. If desired, thicken gravy. *Serves 8.*

Each Serving:	Calories 308 kcal	Protein 34 gm
	Fat 16 gm	Carbohydrate 6 gm
	Sodium 909 mg	Cholesterol 111 mg

 CORN CHOWDER

¾   cup chopped onion
2   tablespoons margarine or butter
1   cup frozen hash brown potatoes
1   cup diced, cooked ham
1   package (10 ounces) frozen corn
1   cup cream-style corn
1   can (10¾ ounces) cream of mushroom soup,
    undiluted
2½ cups milk
    salt
    black pepper
    parsley flakes

Combine onion, margarine, potatoes, ham, corn, cream
of mushroom soup, and milk in Crock-Pot. Cover and
cook on High 4 to 5 hours. Salt and pepper to taste.
Garnish with parsley flakes. Serve. *Serves 8.*

Each Serving:	Calories 224 kcal	Protein 9 gm
	Fat 10 gm	Carbohydrate 26 gm
	Sodium 740 mg	Cholesterol 21 mg

POTATO AND MUSHROOM CHOWDER

This delightful recipe contains a rich broth and a variety of vegetables that sets this chowder apart from others.

½	cup chopped onion
¼	cup margarine or butter
2	tablespoons all-purpose flour
1	teaspoon salt
½	teaspoon black pepper
2	cups water
2	cans (4 ounce each) sliced mushrooms, drained
1	cup chopped celery
2	cups diced peeled potatoes
1	cup chopped carrots
2	cups milk
¼	cup grated Parmesan cheese

In a skillet, sauté onion and celery in the 1/4 cup margarine until the onion is translucent. Remove from heat. Add flour, salt, and pepper; stir. Place in Crock-Pot. Add water. Then stir in potatoes, canned mushrooms, and carrots. Cover and cook on Low 6 to 8 hours or on High for 3 to 4 hours. If on Low turn to High. Add milk and Parmesan cheese and cook 30 minutes. Serve.

Shortcut: Use 2 cups frozen hash browns and 1 cup frozen carrots and cook on High for 2 to 3 hours.

Each Serving:	Calories 204 kcal	Protein 6 gm
	Fat 12 gm	Carbohydrate 20 gm
	Sodium 673 mg	Cholesterol 14 mg

NABIL'S GRECIAN BEEF STEW

2	pounds lean stewing beef, cut into 1½-inch cubes
2	onions, sliced
2	cloves garlic, chopped
2	tablespoons vegetable oil
1	eggplant (unpeeled), cubed
1	cup beef broth
2½	teaspoons cinnamon
1	teaspoon salt
	pepper
1	can (16 ounces) garbanzos, drained
1	can (16 ounces) tomato wedges, drained
1	tablespoon Kitchen Bouquet
	fluffy rice
	minced parsley

In large skillet, brown beef, onions and garlic in oil; drain. Place in Crock-Pot.

Parboil eggplant in 2 cups boiling, salted water for 2 minutes; drain. Add to beef mixture; stir well. Combine beef broth with cinnamon, salt and pepper and pour into Crock-Pot; stir well. Cover and cook on Low for 10 to 12 hours.

One hour before serving, stir in garbanzos, tomato wedges and Kitchen Bouquet. *Serves 4 to 6.*

Each Serving:	Calories 515 kcal	Protein 43 gm
	Fat 20 gm	Carbohydrate 40 gm
	Sodium 1,340 mg	Cholesterol 118 mg

LAMB STEW WITH VEGETABLES

3	pounds boneless lamb stewing meat, well trimmed
1/2	cup flour
1	teaspoon salt
1	teaspoon sugar
1/2	teaspoon leaf thyme
1/4	teaspoon pepper
1/4	teaspoon garlic powder (optional)
1	can (14 ounces) beef broth
3-4	potatoes, peeled and cubed
3	large carrots, pared and thinly sliced
6-8	small white onions
1	package (10 ounces) frozen peas

Wipe off any collected juices from lamb. Combine flour with salt, sugar, thyme, pepper and garlic powder; toss with lamb to coat thoroughly. Place all ingredients except peas in Crock-Pot; stir well. Cover and cook on Low for 10 to 12 hours. One hour before serving, turn to High and stir in frozen peas. Cover and cook until done. *Serves 6 to 8.*

Note: Peas may be added at beginning of cooking, but will darken slightly.

Each Serving:	Calories 712 kcal	Protein 83 gm
	Fat 18 gm	Carbohydrate 52 gm
	Sodium 662 mg	Cholesterol 210 mg

SPAGHETTI MEAT SAUCE

1/2	pound sweet or hot Italian link sausage
1	pound ground chuck
1	pound round steak or stewing beef, cut into 1-inch cubes
2	medium onions, chopped
1	large green pepper, seeded and chopped
2	cloves garlic, minced
2	tablespoons sugar
1	tablespoon salt
2	teaspoons leaf basil
1/8	teaspoon crushed red pepper
2	cans (16 ounces each) Italian-style tomatoes, broken up
1	can (8 ounces) tomato sauce
1	can (6 ounces) tomato paste

Remove sausage from casings; brown in skillet with ground chuck and cubed meat. Break up sausage and ground meat with wooden spoon or fork as they brown; drain well. Add to Crock-Pot with remaining ingredients; stir well. Cover and cook on Low for 8 to 16 hours or on High for 4 to 6 hours. For thicker sauce, cook on High for last 2 hours, removing cover for last hour.

Note: This sauce may be made 1 to 2 days in advance and refrigerated. It also freezes well.

Each Serving:	Calories 336 kcal	Protein 25 gm
	Fat 19 gm	Carbohydrate 17 gm
	Sodium 1,425 mg	Cholesterol 77 mg

CHICKEN-MUSHROOM PASTA SAUCE

2-3	pound fryer, whole or cut up
2	stalks celery, sliced
2	onions, chopped
1	teaspoon salt
1/2	cup chicken broth or water
1	can (6 ounces) tomato paste
1/4	cup dry sherry
1	teaspoon leaf oregano
1	pound mushrooms, sliced, or 2 cans (4 ounces each) sliced mushrooms, drained
2	tablespoons butter
2	tablespoons flour
1/2	cup heavy cream or half-and-half cream

Place fryer in Crock-Pot with celery, onions and salt. Combine chicken broth with tomato paste and pour over ingredients in Crock-Pot. Add sherry, oregano and mushrooms; stir to moisten all ingredients. Cover and cook on Low for 8 to 10 hours or on High for 3½ to 5 hours.

Remove chicken; bone meat and dice. Return meat to Crock-Pot. Knead butter and flour together and add with cream; stir well. Cover and cook on High for 30 minutes to 1½ hours or on Low for 3 to 5 hours. *Serves 4 to 6.*

Each Serving: Calories 349 kcal   Protein 29 gm
                    Fat 18 gm   Carbohydrate 21 gm
                    Sodium 969 mg   Cholesterol 121 mg

FRESH TOMATO SAUCE

4	cups peeled, seeded and finely chopped tomatoes
1	medium onion, minced
1½	teaspoons leaf basil
1	teaspoon sugar
1	can (6 ounces) tomato paste
3	cloves garlic, crushed

Combine all ingredients in lightly oiled Crock-Pot. Cover and cook on Low for 6 to 12 hours or on High for 4 hours. If a thicker sauce is desired, remove cover and cook on High until sauce is reduced.

This is good used in any recipe calling for tomato sauce.

About 5 cups. Double recipe for 5-quart Crock-Pot.

Each Serving:	Calories 79 kcal	Protein 3 gm
	Fat <1 gm	Carbohydrate 18 gm
	Sodium 283 mg	Cholesterol 0 mg

MARINARA SAUCE

2   **cans (28 ounces each) whole tomatoes**
1   **onion, finely chopped**
2   **carrots, pared and finely chopped**
1   **clove garlic, chopped**
2   **tablespoons vegetable oil**
1½   **teaspoons sugar**
1½   **teaspoons salt**

Place tomatoes in batches in blender container; blend until smooth (or puree tomatoes through a food mill).

In skillet, sauté onion, carrots and garlic in oil just until tender (do not brown). Combine all ingredients in Crock-Pot; stir well. Cover and cook on Low for 6 to 10 hours. Remove cover, stir well and cook on High for the last hour for a thicker marinara sauce. *About 6 cups.*

Each Serving: Calories 119 kcal   Protein 3 gm
               Fat 5 gm   Carbohydrate 17 gm
               Sodium 990 mg   Cholesterol 0 mg

Beans, Rice and Pasta

SPICY RICE CASSEROLE

- 2 pounds mild bulk pork sausage
- 2 teaspoons ground cumin
- 1 teaspoon garlic powder
- 4 medium onions, chopped
- 4 medium green peppers, chopped
- 4 beef bouillon cubes
- 4 cups boiling water
- 3 jalapeño peppers, seeded and minced
- 2 packages (6¼ ounces each) converted long grain and wild rice mix

Pour hot water into Crock-Pot which has been set to High. Stir in bouillon cubes. Brown sausage, garlic powder, and cumin in skillet. Drain. Add onions and green peppers, sauté until tender (15 to 20 minutes). Transfer to Crock-Pot. Stir in jalapeño peppers and rice.

Cover and cook on High for 1 hour, then turn to Low and cook 1 to 2 more hours. Serve. *Serves 10 to 12.*

Note: If a spicier rice casserole is desired add seasoning mix that is included with rice.

Each Serving:	Calories 285 kcal	Protein 12 gm
	Fat 13 gm	Carbohydrate 32 gm
	Sodium 1,167 mg	Cholesterol 32 mg

BEAN CASSEROLE

- 1 can (16 ounces) pork and beans, undrained
- 3 cans (16 ounces each) pork and beans, drained
- ¾ cup chopped onion

1 cup shredded sharp cheddar cheese
1 tablespoon + 1 teaspoon chili powder
4 tablespoons Worcestershire sauce
4 tablespoons brown sugar
2 tablespoons white vinegar
1 tablespoon prepared mustard
8 slices bacon, fried and crumbled

Lightly grease Crock-Pot. Combine beans, onion, cheese, chili powder, Worcestershire sauce, brown sugar, vinegar, and mustard in Crock-Pot. Top with crumbled bacon. Cover and cook on Low 6 to 8 hours or on High 3 to 4 hours. Serve. *Serves 8 to 10.*

Each Serving:	Calories 295 kcal	Protein 11 gm
	Fat 11 gm	Carbohydrate 43 gm
	Sodium 983 mg	Cholesterol 32 mg

OUR BEST BAKED BEANS

5 slices bacon, crisply fried and crumbled
2 cans (16 ounces each) baked beans, drained
1/2 green pepper, seeded and chopped
1/2 medium onion, chopped
1 1/2 teaspoons prepared mustard
1/2 cup ketchup
1/2 cup hickory-smoke barbecue sauce
1/2 cup brown sugar (packed)

Mix all ingredients in Crock-Pot. Cover and cook on Low for 8 to 12 hours or on High for 3 to 4 hours. *Serves 6 to 8.*

Each Serving:	Calories 253 kcal	Protein 9 gm
	Fat 4 gm	Carbohydrate 49 gm
	Sodium 1,014 mg	Cholesterol 13 mg

OLD-FASHIONED BAKED BEANS

1   pound dried pea (navy) beans
1   medium onion, finely chopped
½   cup ketchup
½   cup brown sugar (packed)
½   cup dark corn syrup
1   teaspoon paprika
½   teaspoon leaf basil
    salt
1   pound smoked ham, bacon or salt pork, diced

Completely soften beans as directed below. Drain and stir in remaining ingredients. Pour into Crock-Pot. Cover and cook on Low for 6 to 12 hours or on High for 3 to 4 hours. *Serves 8.*

Each Serving:	Calories 401 kcal	Protein 24 gm
	Fat 4 gm	Carbohydrate 70 gm
	Sodium 1,037 mg	Cholesterol 27 mg

A BIT ABOUT BEANS

Cooking with dried beans can be tricky, even in a Crock-Pot. The minerals in the water and variations in voltage affect different types of beans in different ways. For best results, keep these points in mind:

● Dried beans, especially red kidney beans, should be boiled before adding to a recipe. Cover the beans with 3 times their volume of unsalted water and bring to a boil. Boil 10 minutes, and reduce heat.

● Beans must be softened completely before combining with sugar and/or acid foods. (Note: sugar and acid have a hardening effect on beans and will prevent softening.) After boiling beans 10 minutes, reduce heat, cover and allow to simmer 1½ hours or until beans are tender. Soaking in water, if desired, should be completed before boiling. Discard water after soaking or boiling.

SPICY WESTERN BEANS

This zesty bean recipe is full with the flavor of chili peppers and the extra taste of lentils makes a great side dish for any potluck dinner or picnic.

1/3	cup lentils
1 1/3	cups water
4	bacon strips, fried and diced
1	onion, chopped
2	tablespoons ketchup
1	teaspoon garlic powder
3/4	teaspoon chili powder
1/2	teaspoon ground cumin
1/4	teaspoon dried red pepper flakes
	bay leaf
1	14 ounce can whole tomatoes with liquid, chopped
1	can (16 ounces) pinto beans with liquid
1	can (16 ounces) red kidney beans with liquid

Boil 1/3 cup lentils in 1 1/3 cup water for 20 to 30 minutes. Drain. Fry bacon strips. In bacon grease, cook onions until transparent. Combine lentils, bacon, onion, ketchup, garlic powder, chili powder, cumin, pepper flakes, bay leaf, tomatoes, and beans in Crock-Pot. Cook on High 3 to 4 hours. Remove bay leaf. Serve. *Serves 8 to 10.*

Each Serving:	Calories 183 kcal	Protein 9 gm
	Fat 6 gm	Carbohydrate 24 gm
	Sodium 569 mg	Cholesterol 7 mg

BEAN AND CORNBREAD CASSEROLE

1	medium onion, chopped
1	medium green pepper, chopped
2	cloves garlic minced or $\frac{1}{4}$ teaspoon garlic powder
1	can (16 ounces) red kidney beans, undrained
1	can (16 ounces) pinto beans, undrained
1	can (16 ounces) no-salt-added diced tomatoes, undrained
1	can (8 ounces) no-salt-added tomato sauce
1	teaspoon chili powder
$\frac{1}{2}$	teaspoon black pepper
$\frac{1}{2}$	teaspoon prepared mustard
$\frac{1}{8}$	teaspoon hot sauce
1	cup yellow cornmeal
1	cup all-purpose flour
$2\frac{1}{2}$	teaspoons baking powder
$\frac{1}{2}$	teaspoon salt
1	tablespoon sugar
$1\frac{1}{4}$	cups milk
$\frac{1}{2}$	cup egg substitute
3	tablespoons vegetable oil
1	can ($8\frac{1}{2}$ ounces) no-salt-added cream-style corn

Lightly grease Crock-Pot. In a skillet over medium heat, cook onion and green pepper until tender. Transfer to Crock-Pot. Stir in kidney beans and pinto beans. Add diced tomatoes, tomato sauce, seasonings, and hot sauce. Cover and cook on High for 1 hour.

In a mixing bowl, combine cornmeal, flour, baking

powder, salt and sugar. Stir in milk, egg substitute, vegetable oil and cream-style corn. Spoon evenly over bean mixture; may have left over cornbread depending on size of Crock-Pot being used (if have remaining cornbread, spoon into greased muffin tins and bake at 375° for 30 minutes or until golden brown). Cover and cook on High for 1½ to 2 more hours. Serve. *Serves 6 to 8.*

Each Serving: Calories 404 kcal   Protein 15 gm
                 Fat 9 gm   Carbohydrate 67 gm
                 Sodium 904 mg   Cholesterol 6 mg

BEEF 'N BEANS

1	pound dried pinto beans
¼	pound salt pork or bacon, diced
1-2	pound chuck steak, cut into 1-inch cubes
⅛-¼	teaspoon crushed red pepper
2	cloves garlic, minced
1	can (6 ounces) tomato paste
1	cup water
1	tablespoon chili powder
	salt
1	teaspoon ground cumin

Completely soften beans as directed on page 162. In skillet, brown salt pork and cubed chuck steak over medium-heat; drain well. Add to Crock-Pot with soaked pinto beans. Add remaining ingredients; stir well. Cover and cook on High for 2 hours, then on Low for 7 to 12 hours or cook entire time on High for 5 to 8 hours. *Serves 8.*

Each Serving: Calories 538 kcal   Protein 28 gm
                 Fat 30 gm   Carbohydrate 41 gm
                 Sodium 443 mg   Cholesterol 74 mg

CRACKED WHEAT PILAF

2 cups cracked wheat or bulgur
1 medium onion, chopped
5 cups beef broth
¼ cup butter, melted
¼ cup minced parsley or 2 tablespoons dried parsley flakes
   salt

Combine all ingredients in Crock-Pot; stir well. Cover and cook on Low for 10 to 12 hours or on High for 3 to 4 hours, stirring occasionally. *Serves 6 to 8.*

Each Serving:	Calories 219 kcal	Protein 6 gm
	Fat 8 gm	Carbohydrate 33 gm
	Sodium 1,247 mg	Cholesterol 18 mg

BURGER 'N BEAN HOT DISH

1 pound ground beef
1 can (16 ounces) barbecue beans
1 can (11½ ounces) condensed bean with bacon soup
⅛ teaspoon seasoned black pepper
¼ teaspoon chili powder
½ teaspoon garlic salt
1 tablespoon instant minced onion
½ cup grated process American cheese

In skillet, brown ground beef; drain well. Thoroughly combine all ingredients except cheese in Crock-Pot. Cover and cook on Low for 6 to 9 hours.

Just before serving, sprinkle with grated cheese. Serve over hot corn bread. *Serves 6.*

Each Serving:	Calories 350 kcal	Protein 21 gm
	Fat 18 gm	Carbohydrate 24 gm
	Sodium 986 mg	Cholesterol 56 mg

DRIED BEEF 'N NOODLES

3-4 ounces dried beef
1 package (8 ounces) noodles
2 teaspoons vegetable oil
¼ cup butter or margarine
¼ cup flour
2 cups evaporated milk
1 package (10 ounces) frozen peas or frozen mixed vegetables, partially thawed
1 package (8 ounces) sharp process cheese, grated

Snip dried beef into small pieces; set aside. Cook noodles according to package directions until barely tender. In large bowl, toss with oil; set aside. In saucepan, melt butter over medium heat. Blend in flour until smooth. Gradually stir in evaporated milk. Cook until smooth and thick.

Pour white sauce over noodles; toss to mix. Fold in snipped beef, vegetables and most of grated cheese, reserving a small amount to sprinkle over top; stir well. Pour mixture into well-greased Crock-Pot. Sprinkle lightly with reserved cheese. Cover and cook on Low for 6 to 10 hours. *Serves 4 to 6.*

Each Serving:	Calories 675 kcal	Protein 33 gm
	Fat 36 gm	Carbohydrate 56 gm
	Sodium 1,611 mg	Cholesterol 140 mg

POLENTA/CORNMEAL MUSH

2-4	tablespoons butter or margarine, melted
1/4	teaspoon paprika
	dash cayenne pepper
6	cups boiling water
2	cups cornmeal (preferably water ground)
1	teaspoon salt

Use 1 tablespoon butter to lightly grease walls of Crock-Pot. Add paprika and cayenne. Turn to High while measuring remaining ingredients. Add to Crock-Pot with remaining melted butter; stir well. Cover and cook on Low for 6 to 9 hours or on High for 2 to 3 hours, stirring occasionally. *Serves 8 to 10.*

Fried Polenta or Cornmeal Mush: Pour hot cornmeal into 2 lightly greased loaf pans. Chill overnight. To serve, cut into 3/4-inch slices and fry in butter until browned.

Each Serving:	Calories 121 kcal	Protein 2 gm
	Fat 4 gm	Carbohydrate 21 gm
	Sodium 299 mg	Cholesterol 0 mg

BEAN POTPOURRI

2	cans (15 ounces each) garbanzos
1	can (16 ounces) pinto beans, undrained
4	medium potatoes, peeled and diced
1	large onion, thinly sliced
1	teaspoon salt
3	slices bacon, crisply fried and crumbled

1   pound cross-cut beef shank

$\frac{1}{2}$ pound smoked ham hock

3-4   ounces Polish sausage or knockwurst, thinly sliced

$2\frac{1}{2}$ cups water

Combine all ingredients in Crock-Pot; stir well. Cover and cook on Low for 8 to 16 hours or on High for 4 to 6 hours. *Serves 8 to 10.*

Each Serving:	Calories 328 kcal	Protein 20 gm
	Fat 9 gm	Carbohydrate 41 gm
	Sodium 1,338 mg	Cholesterol 30 mg

SAUSAGE BEAN QUICKIE

4-6   cooked brown 'n serve sausage links, cut into 1-inch pieces

2   teaspoons cider vinegar

2   cans (16 ounces each) red kidney or baked beans, drained

1   can (7 ounces) pineapple chunks, undrained

2   teaspoons brown sugar

3   tablespoons flour

Combine sausage, vinegar, beans and pineapple in Crock-Pot. Mix brown sugar with flour and add; stir well. Cover and cook on Low for 7 to 10 hours or on High for 2 to 3 hours. *Serves 4.*

Each Serving:	Calories 284 kcal	Protein 15 gm
	Fat 7 gm	Carbohydrate 41 gm
	Sodium 414 mg	Cholesterol 11 mg

RED RICE

5 slices bacon, fried and crumbled
1 large onion, chopped
2 cans (16 ounces each) chopped, peeled
   tomatoes, undrained
1 cup converted long-grain rice, uncooked
1 cup finely chopped cooked ham
½ teaspoon salt
¼ teaspoon black pepper
⅛ teaspoon hot sauce

Fry bacon in skillet and set aside. Cook onion in drippings over medium-high heat until tender. Combine bacon, onion, tomatoes, rice, ham, and seasonings in Crock-Pot. Cover and cook on Low 6 to 8 hours or on High 3 to 4 hours. Serve. *Serves 6 to 8.*

If hotter rice is desired, add more hot sauce to taste.

Each Serving:	Calories 262 kcal	Protein 9 gm
	Fat 12 gm	Carbohydrate 30 gm
	Sodium 783 mg	Cholesterol 23 mg

ARROZ CON QUESO

1½ cups raw long-grain converted rice
1   can (16 ounces) whole tomatoes, mashed
1   can (16 ounces) Mexican-style beans
3   cloves garlic, minced
1   large onion, finely chopped
2   tablespoons vegetable oil
1   cup cottage cheese
1   can (4 ounces) green chili peppers, drained,
    seeded and chopped
2   cups grated Monterey Jack or process cheese

Mix thoroughly all ingredients except 1 cup of the grated cheese. Pour mixture into well-greased Crock-Pot. Cover and cook on Low for 6 to 9 hours.

Just before serving, sprinkle with reserved grated cheese. *Serves 6 to 8.*

Each Serving:	Calories 421 kcal	Protein 19 gm
	Fat 16 gm	Carbohydrate 51 gm
	Sodium 753 mg	Cholesterol 39 mg

BROWN-AND-WHITE RICE

- 8 slices bacon, diced
- 1/2 cup raw brown rice
- 4 green onions with tops, sliced
- 1 can (4 ounces) sliced mushrooms, drained
- 1 cup raw long-grain converted rice
- 3 cups beef broth
- 1/3 cup slivered almonds, toasted
- 3 tablespoons grated Parmesan cheese

In skillet, fry bacon until partially crisp but still limp. Stir in brown rice and cook over medium heat until rice is a light golden brown. Add bacon and browned rice to Crock-Pot with green onions, mushrooms, white rice and broth; stir well. Cover and cook on Low for 6 to 8 hours or on High for 2½ to 3½ hours. Before serving, stir well; add salt if needed. Garnish with almonds and cheese. *Serves 6 to 8.*

Each Serving:	Calories 352 kcal	Protein 8 gm
	Fat 20 gm	Carbohydrate 34 gm
	Sodium 962 mg	Cholesterol 19 mg

SAUSAGE-RICE CASSEROLE

1 **pound bulk sausage**
1 **envelope (1½ ounces) dry chicken soup mix**
¾ **cup raw long-grain converted rice**
2 **stalks celery, diced**
⅓ **cup slivered almonds**
4 **cups water**
   salt

In skillet, brown sausage; drain well. Combine all ingredients in lightly greased Crock-Pot; stir well. Cover and cook on Low for 7 to 10 hours or on High for 3 to 4 hours or until rice is tender. *Serves 4.*

Each Serving:	Calories 687 kcal	Protein 18 gm
	Fat 53 gm	Carbohydrate 34 gm
	Sodium 2,282 mg	Cholesterol 77 mg

GOLDEN CHEESE BAKE

2 **cups cooked long-grain converted rice**
3 **cups pared and grated carrots**
2 **cups grated sharp process cheese**
½ **cup milk**
2 **eggs, beaten**
2 **tablespoons chopped onion**
1 **teaspoon salt**
¼ **teaspoon pepper**

In bowl, combine all ingredients; stir well. Pour into greased Crock-Pot. Cover and cook on Low for 7 to 9 hours or on High for 2½ to 3 hours.

Serves 4 to 6. Double recipe for 5-quart Crock-Pot.

Each Serving:	Calories 325 kcal	Protein 16 gm
	Fat 17 gm	Carbohydrate 27 gm
	Sodium 1,152 mg	Cholesterol 131 mg

MONTEREY SPAGHETTI

This tasty side dish is a hit with any main meal.

- 4 ounces spaghetti, broken into 2-inch pieces
- 1 egg
- 1 cup sour cream
- ¼ cup grated Parmesan cheese
- ¼ teaspoon garlic powder
- 3 cups shredded Monterey Jack cheese
- 1 package (10 ounces) frozen chopped spinach, thawed and drained
- 1 can (3 ounces) french fried onions

Grease Crock-Pot. Cook spaghetti in boiling water for 5 to 7 minutes. Drain. In a small bowl, beat egg. Transfer to the Crock-Pot. Add sour cream, Parmesan cheese, and garlic powder. Mix spaghetti, 2 cups Monterey Jack cheese, spinach and half of the onions in the Crock-Pot. Cover and cook on Low 6 to 8 hours or on High for 3 to 4 hours. In the last 30 minutes of cooking turn to High if cooking on Low and add to top of casserole the remainder of Monterey Jack cheese and the onions. Serve when cheese is melted. *Serves 6 to 8.*

Each Serving:	Calories 377 kcal	Protein 19 gm
	Fat 26 gm	Carbohydrate 17 gm
	Sodium 391 mg	Cholesterol 99 mg

WILD RICE CASEROLE

$1/2$ cup butter or margarine, melted
  3 stalks celery, thinly sliced
  2 medium onions, finely chopped
  1 can ($10^3/4$ ounces) condensed cream of mushroom soup
$2^1/2$ cups water
  2 packages (7 ounces each) wild rice and long-grain converted rice mix
  1 can (4 ounces) sliced mushrooms, drained
$1/2$ pound process American cheese, cubed

Combine all ingredients in Crock-Pot; stir thoroughly. Cover and cook on Low for 6 to 10 hours or on High for 2 to $3^1/2$ hours. *Serves 6 to 8.*

Each Serving:	Calories 494 kcal	Protein 15 gm
	Fat 21 gm	Carbohydrate 51 gm
	Sodium 1,951 mg	Cholesterol 31 mg

SPINACH NOODLE CASSEROLE

  1 package (8 ounces) spinach noodles
  2 tablespoons vegetable oil or melted butter
$1^1/2$ cups (12 ounces) sour cream
$1/3$ cup flour
$1^1/2$ cups small-curd cream-style cottage cheese
  4 green onions with tops, finely minced
  2 teaspoons Worcestershire sauce

dash Tabasco sauce
2 teaspoons garlic salt

Cook noodles according to package directions until barely tender. Rinse in cold water and drain. Toss with oil. In large bowl, mix sour cream and flour. Stir in remaining ingredients. Add noodles and stir well to coat. Pour into well-greased Crock-Pot. Cover and cook on High for 1½ to 2½ hours. If desired, serve with additional sour cream. *8 servings.*

Each Serving:	Calories 264 kcal	Protein 11 gm
	Fat 13 gm	Carbohydrate 26 gm
	Sodium 770 mg	Cholesterol 21 mg

MACARONI AND BEEF

1½ pounds lean ground beef
2 cups uncooked macaroni
½ medium onion, chopped
1 can (4 ounces) sliced mushrooms, drained
1 can (16 ounces) whole-kernel corn, drained
2 cans (10¾ ounces each) condensed tomato soup
salt and pepper

In skillet, brown ground beef; drain well. Put into Crock-Pot. Cook macaroni according to package directions until barely tender; drain well. Add macaroni and remaining ingredients to Crock-Pot. Stir just enough to blend. Cover and cook on Low for 7 to 9 hours or on High for 3 to 4 hours. *Serves 4 to 6.*

Each Serving:	Calories 590 kcal	Protein 34 gm
	Fat 22 gm	Carbohydrate 67 gm
	Sodium 1,226 mg	Cholesterol 82 mg

MACARONI AND CHEESE

3   cups cooked macaroni
1   tablespoon butter or margarine, melted
2   cups evaporated milk
3   cups shredded sharp process cheese
¼   cup finely chopped green pepper
¼   cup chopped onion
1   teaspoon salt
¼   teaspoon pepper

Toss macaroni with butter or margarine. Add remaining ingredients. Pour into lightly greased Crock-Pot. Cover and cook on High 2 to 3 hours, stirring once or twice.

Each Serving:	Calories 445 kcal	Protein 22 gm
	Fat 27 gm	Carbohydrate 30 gm
	Sodium 1,288 mg	Cholesterol 83 mg

SPAGHETTI WITH MEATBALLS

2   tablespoons olive oil or butter
1   clove garlic, minced
1   medium onion, finely chopped
1   can (28 ounces) Italian-style tomatoes, mashed
2   teaspoons salt
½   teaspoon sugar
1   teaspoon leaf basil
1   teaspoon leaf oregano
1   can (6 ounces) tomato paste
¼   teaspoon crushed red pepper

Meatballs (below)(optional)
2   packages (16 ounces each) spaghetti
    grated Parmesan cheese

Combine all ingredients except Meatballs, spaghetti and
cheese in Crock-Pot; stir well. Cover and cook on Low for
5 to 10 hours. If Meatballs are added, continue to cook on
Low for 7 to 12 hours.

Just before serving, cook spaghetti according to package
directions. Serve topped with Meatballs in sauce and pass
grated Parmesan cheese. *Serves 10 to 12.*

Meatballs:
1   pound lean ground beef
1/2 pound lean ground pork
1   teaspoon garlic salt
1/4 cup grated Parmesan cheese
1/8 teaspoon freshly ground pepper
1/2 teaspoon leaf basil
1/2 teaspoon leaf oregano
1/4 teaspoon leaf thyme
3/4 cup dry bread crumbs
1/3 cup pine nuts (optional)
2   tablespoons dried parsley flakes
2   eggs
1/4 cup evaporated milk

Mix all ingredients thoroughly. Shape into 24 meatballs
about 1½ inches in diameter. Place on baking sheet and
bake in 450° oven for 15 to 20 minutes or brown
meatballs in skillet; drain.

Each Serving:	Calories 559 kcal	Protein 25 gm
	Fat 17 gm	Carbohydrate 76 gm
	Sodium 721 mg	Cholesterol 82 mg

HUNGARIAN NOODLE SIDE DISH

3 chicken bouillon cubes
1/4 cup boiling water
1 can (10¾ ounces) cream of mushroom soup
1/2 cup chopped onion
2 tablespoons Worcestershire sauce
1 tablespoon poppy seeds
1/4 teaspoon garlic powder
1/4 teaspoon hot pepper sauce
2 cups cottage cheese
2 cups sour cream
1 package (16 ounces) wide egg noodles, cooked and drained
1/4 cup shredded Parmesan cheese
Paprika

Lightly grease Crock-Pot. Cook noodles in boiling water for 5 to 7 minutes; drain. In a large bowl, dissolve bouillon in water. Add the next six ingredients. Stir in cottage cheese, sour cream, and noodles. Transfer to Crock-Pot. Sprinkle with Parmesan cheese and paprika. Cover and cook on High 3 to 4 hours. Serve immediately. *Serves 8 to 10.*

Each Serving:	Calories 415 kcal	Protein 17 gm
	Fat 19 gm	Carbohydrate 44 gm
	Sodium 912 mg	Cholesterol 80¡ mg

VEGETABLES AND SIDE DISHES

SWEET POTATO CASSEROLE

This casserole is excellent to make for the holidays, by using the Crock-Pot Slow Cooker it frees your oven for other dishes

- 2   cans (18 ounces each) sweet potatoes, mashed
- 1/3 cup margarine or butter, melted
- 2   tablespoons sugar
- 2   tablespoons brown sugar
- 1   tablespoon orange juice
- 2   eggs, beaten
- 1/2 cup milk
- 1/3 cup chopped pecans
- 1/3 cup brown sugar
- 2   tablespoons all-purpose flour
- 2   tablespoons margarine or butter, melted

Lightly grease Crock-Pot. Mix sweet potatoes, 1/3 cup margarine, sugar, and brown sugar. Beat in orange juice, eggs, milk. Transfer to Crock-Pot.

Combine pecans, 1/3 cup brown sugar, flour, and 2 tablespoons margarine. Spread over sweet potatoes.

Cover and cook on High 3 to 4 hours. Serve. *Serves 6 to 8.*

CHEESE POTATO PUFF

- 12 medium potatoes, peeled and quartered
- 1   teaspoon salt, divided
- 3/4 cup margarine or butter, melted
- 2   cups shredded cheddar cheese
- 1   cup milk
- 2   eggs, beaten
     dried chives for garnish

Lightly grease Crock-Pot. Place potatoes in large sauce-pan with 1/2 teaspoon salt; cover with water and boil until tender (15 minutes). Drain, then mash. Transfer to Crock-Pot. Stir in margarine, cheese, milk, and 1/2 teaspoon salt. Cover and cook on High 3 to 4 hours. Top with chives if desired. Serve immediately. *Serves 10 to 12.*

CREAM CHEESE POTATOES

- 2 tablespoons dried onion, minced or chopped
- 2 cloves garlic, minced or 1/4 teaspoon garlic powder
- 1 teaspoon salt
- 1/4 teaspoon black pepper
- 8 medium potatoes, scrubbed and sliced (about 2 pounds)
- 1 package (8 ounces) cream cheese, cut in cubes

Lightly grease Crock-Pot. In a small bowl, combine onion, garlic, salt, and pepper. Layer 1/4 of the sliced potatoes in the bottom of the Crock-Pot. Sprinkle with 1/4 of season-ings. Layer with 1/3 of cream cheese cubes. Continue layer-ing process, ending with a layer of potatoes then sprinkle with seasonings. Cover and cook on High 3 to 4 hours. In the last hour of cooking stir the potatoes to distribute the cream cheese. Serve when potatoes are tender.

Note: If desired, potatoes can be slightly mashed prior to serving. *Serves 4 to 6.*

TIME SAVING TIPS

1. Cook potatoes in boiling water to cover for about 30 minutes or until tender and then cut into strips. Then mixture should be cooked on low for 6 – 8 hours or on high for about 2 hours, again until potatoes are tender.

2. Substitute 32 oz. of frozen hashbrowns for potatoes and prepare as mentioned above. Cook on low 4– 6 hours or 2 hours on high.

SCALLOPED POTATOES

1/2	cup margarine or butter, melted
1/4	cup dried, chopped onions
1	package (16 ounces) frozen hash brown potatoes
1	can (10¾ ounces) cream of mushroom soup
1½	cups milk
1	cup shredded cheddar cheese
1	small green pepper, cut into small pieces
2	tablespoons chopped pimiento
1/8	teaspoon black pepper
1	cup cheese cracker crumbs, divided

Lightly grease Crock-Pot. Stir together margarine, onions, hash brown potatoes, cream of mushroom soup, milk, cheese, green pepper, pimiento, black pepper, and ½ cup cracker crumbs. Transfer to Crock-Pot. Top with remaining cracker crumbs. Cover and cook on High for 3 to 4 hours. Serve. *Serves 6 to 8.*

CHEESY POTATO CASSEROLE

7	medium potatoes (about 2 pounds)
¼	cup butter or margarine melted
1	small onion chopped or 1 tablespoon minced onion
1	teaspoon salt
1	carton (8 ounces) sour cream
1	can (10¾ ounces) cream of chicken soup
2	cups shredded cheddar cheese
3	tablespoons butter or margarine, melted
1½-2	cups herb-seasoning stuffing mix

Peel and cut potatoes into ¼-inch strips; set aside.

Combine ¼ cup melted margarine, onion, salt, pepper, sour cream, and cream of chicken soup in a bowl.

Lightly butter inside of 5-quart Crock-Pot and place potatoes inside. Mix 2 cups of shredded cheddar cheese with potatoes. Pour sour cream/soup mixture into potatoes and mix well. Cover top of potato mixture with the stuffing mix and drizzle with the 3 tablespoons melted margarine. Cover cook on Low for 8 to 10 hours until potatoes are tender or 5 to 6 hours on High.

TIME SAVING TIPS

1. Cook potatoes in boiling water to cover for about 30 minutes or until tender and then cut into strips. Then mixture should be cooked on low for 6 – 8 hours or on high for about 2 hours, again until potatoes are tender.

2. Substitute 32 oz. of frozen hasbrowns for potatoes and prepare as mentioned above. Cook on low 4– 6 hours or 2 hours on high.

ASPARAGUS CASSEROLE

2   packages (10 ounces each) frozen asparagus
    spears, thawed
1   can (10¾ ounces) condensed cream of celery
    soup
1   can (10¾ ounces) condensed cream of
    chicken soup
2   cups crushed saltine crackers
1   cup cubed process American cheese
1   egg
½   cup slivered almonds

In large bowl, combine all ingredients well. Pour into
lightly greased Crock-Pot. Cover and cook on High for 3
to 3½ hours.

After cooking, dish may be held on Low for up to 2
hours before serving. *Serves 4 to 6.*

Note: Two cans (14½ ounces each) asparagus pieces,
drained, may be substituted for frozen asparagus.

CARROTS LYONNAISE

1   chicken bouillon cube
1   cup boiling water
2   onions, sliced
¼   cup butter or margarine
1   tablespoon flour
¼   teaspoon salt
6   carrots, pared and cut into julienne strips
1-2 tablespoons sugar (optional)

Dissolve bouillon cube in boiling water; set aside. In large skillet, sauté onions in butter, stirring to separate rings and prevent browning. Stir flour and salt into slightly cooled bouillon; add to onions and cook until thickened. Combine carrots and onion sauce in Crock-Pot, stirring to coat carrots. Cover and cook on High for 1 hour, then turn to Low for 2 to 6 hours. Before serving, add sugar to taste. *Serves 6 to 8.*

LIMA BEAN CASSEROLE

2   small onions, thinly sliced

3   packages (10 ounces each) frozen baby lima beans, thawed

2   cans (10¾ ounces each) condensed cream of celery soup

2   cans (4 ounces each) sliced mushrooms, undrained

1   jar (2 ounces) chopped pimiento, drained

2   teaspoons salt

⅛   teaspoon pepper

½   teaspoon dill seed

½   cup heavy cream

1   cup grated Parmesan cheese

Combine all ingredients except heavy cream and Parmesan cheese in Crock-Pot; stir well. Cover and cook on Low for 10 to 12 hours. Just before serving, add cream and stir well; sprinkle Parmesan cheese on top. *Serves 8 to 10.*

SWEET-AND-SOUR GREEN BEANS

2 packages (10 ounces each) frozen French-style green beans, partially thawed
4 slices bacon, diced
1 small onion, diced
1 tablespoon flour
1/4 cup water
1/4 cup cider vinegar
2 tablespoons sugar
1/2 teaspoon salt
  dash pepper
1 tablespoon chopped pimiento

Break apart green beans and place in Crock-Pot. In skillet, fry bacon until crisp; remove bacon to absorbent towels to drain. Pour off all but 2 tablespoons bacon drippings from skillet; sauté onion in bacon drippings (do not brown). Dissolve flour in water; stir into bacon drippings and cook until slightly thickened. Combine bacon and remaining ingredients and stir into thickened onion mixture. Pour over green beans and stir well. Cover and cook on High for 1 hour, then turn to Low for 7 to 9 hours. *Serves 6 to 8.*

HARVARD BEETS

1/2 cup sugar
2 tablespoons flour
1/4 cup water
1/4 cup white vinegar
2 cans (16 ounces each) whole beets, drained

Mix sugar and flour; stir in water and vinegar. Place
beets in Crock-Pot. Pour sugar-vinegar mixture over
beets and stir to coat well. Cover and cook on High for 3
to 4 hours. *Serves 4 to 6.*

CREAMED CORN

2 packages (16 ounces each) frozen corn
2 packages (8 ounces each) cream cheese,
    softened and cubed
1 medium onion, chopped
    pepper to taste
    garlic powder to taste

In Crock-Pot, combine corn, cream cheese, onion, pepper,
and garlic powder. Cover; cook on High 2 to 3 hours.
Serves 10.

GOLDEN CAULIFLOWER

2   packages (10 ounces each) frozen
    cauliflower, thawed
    salt and pepper
1   can (11 ounces) condensed cheddar cheese
    soup
4   slices bacon, crisply fried and crumbled

Place cauliflower in Crock-Pot. Season with salt and
pepper. Spoon Cheddar cheese soup over top; sprinkle
with bacon. Cover and cook on High for 1½ hours or
cook on Low only for 4 to 5 hours. *Serves 4 to 6.*

Golden Broccoli: Substitute frozen broccoli for the
frozen cauliflower.

CORN PUDDING

This slightly sweet side dish is big in corn taste.

1   8 ounce package cream cheese, softened
2   eggs, beaten
⅓   cup sugar
1   package (8½ ounces) corn bread/muffin mix
1   can (16 ounces) cream-style corn
2⅓ cups fresh or frozen sweet corn
1   cup milk
2   tablespoons margarine or butter, melted
1   teaspoon salt

¹/₄ **teaspoon nutmeg**

Lightly grease Crock-Pot. In a mixing bowl, blend cream cheese, eggs, and sugar. Add the remaining ingredients and mix well. Transfer to Crock-Pot. Cover and cook on High 3 to 4 hours. Serve. *Serves 10 to 12.*

SQUASH CASSEROLE

2 **pounds yellow summer squash or zucchini, thinly sliced (about 6 cups)**
¹/₂ **medium onion, chopped**
1 **cup pared shredded carrot**
1 **can (10³/₄ ounces) condensed cream of chicken soup**
1 **cup sour cream**
¹/₄ **cup flour**
1 **package (8 ounces) seasoned stuffing crumbs**
¹/₂ **cup butter or margarine, melted**

In large bowl, combine squash, onion, carrot and soup. Mix sour cream and flour; stir into vegetables. Toss stuffing crumbs with butter and place half in Crock-Pot. Add vegetable mixture and top with remaining stuffing crumbs. Cover and cook on Low for 6 to 8 hours. *Serves 4 to 6.*

LOUISE'S BROCCOLI CASSEROLE

2   packages (10 ounces each) frozen broccoli
    spears, thawed and cut up
1   can (10¾ ounces) condensed cream of celery
    soup
1¼ cups grated sharp cheddar cheese
¼   cup minced green onion
1   cup crushed saltine crackers or potato chips

In large bowl, combine broccoli, celery soup, 1 cup of the grated cheese and the minced onion. Pour into lightly greased Crock-Pot. Sprinkle top with crushed crackers, then with remaining cheese. Cover and cook on Low for 5 to 6 hours or on High for 2½ to 3 hours). *Serves 4 to 6.*

Note: If desired, casserole may be spooned into a baking dish and garnished with additional grated cheese and broken potato chips; bake for 5 to 10 minutes in a 400° oven.

BREADS, CAKES AND SUCH

WHOLE WHEAT BANANA BREAD

Wheat germ and nuts brings a nutty variation to this Banana Bread recipe.

- ⅔ **cup margarine or butter**
- 1 **cup sugar**
- 2 **eggs**
- 1 **cup mashed bananas, (2-3 bananas)**
- 1 **cup whole wheat flour**
- 1 **cup all–purpose flour**
- ¼ **cup wheat germ**
- 1 **teaspoon baking soda**
- ½ **teaspoon salt**
- ½ **cup chopped pecans or walnuts**

Grease and flour inside of Bread N' Cake Bake Pan.

Cream margarine with an electric mixer. Blend in sugar. Add eggs and mashed bananas. Beat until smooth.

In a small bowl, combine the flours, wheat germ, baking soda, and salt. Add to the creamed mixture. Pour into the prepared Bread N' Cake Bake Pan. Place lid on pan. Put Bread N' Cake Bake Pan in Crock–Pot. Cover Crock–Pot. Cook on High for 3 to 4 hours. Check after 3 hours for doneness. Bread is done when it is pulling away from sides of Bread N' Cake Bake Pan.

When bread is done remove Bread N' Cake Bake Pan from Crock–Pot. Let bread cool then invert bread on plate and then invert bread again for serving.

OLD-FASHIONED APPLE BUTTER

12-14 apples (preferably Jonathan or winesap)
  2   cups apple juice
     sugar
     cinnamon
     allspice
     cloves
 $^1/_2$ cup sauterne (optional)

Wash, core and quarter apples (do not peel). Combine apples and apple juice in lightly oiled Crock-Pot. Cover and cook on Low for 10 to 18 hours or on High for 2 to 4 hours.

When fruit is tender, put through a food mill to remove peel. Measure cooked fruit and return to Crock-Pot. For each pint of sieved cooked fruit, add 1 cup sugar, 1 teaspoon cinnamon, $^1/_2$ teaspoon allspice and $^1/_2$ teaspoon cloves; stir well. Cover and cook on High for 6 to 8 hours, stirring about every 2 hours. Remove cover after 3 hours to allow fruit and juice to cook down. Add sauterne for the last hour off cooking. Spoon into hot sterilized jars and process according to standard canning methods. *About five $^1/_2$-pint jars.*

WHITE BREAD

1   package active dry yeast
1   teaspoon sugar
1/4   cup warm water
1   egg
1/4   cup vegetable oil
1   cup lukewarm water
1   teaspoon salt
1/4   cup sugar
3 1/2-4   cups flour

In large bowl, dissolve yeast and 1 teaspoon sugar in 1/4 cup warm water. Allow to stand until it bubbles and foams. Add egg, oil, lukewarm water, salt, 1/4 cup sugar and 2 cups of the flour. Beat with an electric mixer for 2 minutes. With wooden spoon, stir in remaining 1 1/2 to 2 cups flour until dough leaves the side of the bowl. Place dough in well-greased Bread 'n Cake Bake pan; cover. Place pan in Crock-Pot. Cover and bake on High for 2 to 3 hours or until edges are browned.

Remove pan and uncover. Let stand 5 minutes. Unmold on cake rack. *1 loaf (for 3 1/2- or 5-quart Crock-Pot).*

HONEY WHEAT BREAD

2   cups warm reconstituted dry milk
2   tablespoons vegetable oil
1/4   cup honey
3/4   teaspoon salt
1   package active dry yeast
3   cups whole wheat flour
3/4-1   cup all-purpose flour

Combine warm (not hot) milk, oil, honey, salt, yeast and half the flour. With electric mixer, beat well for about 2 minutes. Add remaining flour; mix well. Place dough in well-greased Bread 'n Cake Bake pan; cover. Let stand for 5 minutes. Place pan in Crock-Pot. Cover and bake on High for 2 to 3 hours.

Remove pan and uncover. Let stand 5 minutes. Unmold and serve warm. *1 loaf (for 3½- or 5-quart Crock-Pot).*

Note: Fresh milk may be used if scalded.

 ## SPOON BREAD, GEORGIA STYLE

1   cup yellow cornmeal
2   teaspoons baking powder
2   eggs
1   cup grated sharp cheese
1   can (17 ounces) cream-style corn
2   tablespoons vegetable oil or butter
1   cup buttermilk
1-2   green chili peppers, seeded and diced

Mix all ingredients well. Pour into greased and floured Bread 'n Cake Bake pan; cover. Place in Crock-Pot. Cover and bake on High for 2 to 3½ hours. Do not unmold. Serve warm, directly from the pan. *Serves 4 to 6 (for 3½- or 5-quart Crock-Pot).*

ORANGE DATE-NUT BREAD

This bread needs no accompaniment simply spread thin slices with butter and serve.

  1 **cup snipped dates**
  4 **teaspoons finely shredded orange peel**
  ²⁄₃ **cup boiling water**
  ¹⁄₃ **cup orange juice**
  ³⁄₄ **cup sugar**
  2 **tablespoons shortening**
  1 **egg, slightly beaten**
  1 **teaspoon vanilla**
  2 **cups flour**
  1 **teaspoon baking powder**
  ¹⁄₂ **teaspoon baking soda**
  ¹⁄₄ **teaspoon salt**
  ¹⁄₂ **cup chopped nuts, such as pecans, walnuts, etc.**

Grease and flour inside of Bread N' Cake Bake Pan.

In a large bowl, combine snipped dates and orange peel. Stir in boiling water and orange juice. Add sugar, shortening, egg, and vanilla, stirring just until mixed.

In a medium bowl, combine flour, baking powder, baking soda, and salt. Add flour mixture to date mixture. Pour into prepared Bread N' Cake Bake Pan. Place cover on Bread N' Cake Bake Pan.

Place Bread N' Cake Bake Pan in Crock-Pot. Cover Crock-Pot and bake on High for 1½ to 2 hours. Check bread after 1½ hours for doneness. Bread is done when sides start pulling away from pan.

PEANUT BUTTER AND HOT FUDGE PUDDING CAKE

Peanut Butter and Chocolate Lover's delight in this luscious hot Pudding Cake.

$1/2$ cup all-purpose flour
$1/4$ cup sugar
$3/4$ teaspoon baking powder
$1/3$ cup milk
 1   tablespoon vegetable oil
$1/2$ teaspoon vanilla
$1/4$ cup peanut butter
$1/2$ cup sugar
 3   tablespoons unsweetened cocoa powder
 1   cup boiling water

In a bowl, combine flour, $1/4$ cup sugar, and baking powder. Add milk, oil, and vanilla; stir until smooth. Mix in peanut butter. Pour into Crock-Pot.

In the same mixing bowl, stir together the $1/2$ cup sugar and cocoa powder. Gradually stir in boiling water. Pour mixture over batter in Crock-Pot. Do not stir.

Cover and cook on High 2 to 3 hours or until a toothpick inserted comes out clean. Serve warm with vanilla ice cream, hot fudge sauce and top with nuts.

HONEY ORANGE AND APPLE NUT BREAD PUDDING

This delicious pudding separates into three distinct layers. Serve warm with a sweetened sour cream.

2	cup all–purpose flour
2/3	cup plus 1/4 cup sugar
3	teaspoons baking powder
1	teaspoon salt
8	tablespoons margarine or butter cut into cubes
1	cup milk
2	medium tart apples, such Granny Smith, peeled cored and cut in cubes
1/2	cup chopped English walnuts
1 1/2	cups orange juice
1/2	cup honey
2	tablespoons margarine or butter, melted
1	teaspoon cinnamon
1 1/3	cups sour cream
4	tablespoons powdered sugar

Lightly grease the inside of the Crock–Pot. In a mixing bowl, mix the flour, the 2/3 cups sugar, the baking powder, and salt. Cut in the margarine with a pastry blender or with 2 knives until the mixture resembles coarse meal. Stir in the milk to form a stiff dough. Spread the dough into the bottom of the Crock–Pot.

Sprinkle the apples and walnuts over the layer of dough. Do not stir.

In another mixing bowl, combine the orange juice, honey, 1/4 cup sugar, the melted margarine, and cinnamon. Pour over the apple mixture. Do not stir.

Cover and cook on High for 2 to 3 hours or until the apples are tender. Do not cook on Low.

In a small bowl, whip the sour cream and powdered sugar.

Serve warm with dollops of the sour cream mixture.

PINEAPPLE BREAD PUDDING

Try this delicious variation to the tried and true Bread Pudding.

1   cup margarine or butter, softened
2   cups sugar
1   teaspoon cinnamon
8   eggs
2   cans (15¼ ounces each) unsweetened crushed pineapple, drained
5   cups toasted bread cubes
     chopped pecans, optional
     whipped cream, optional

In a bowl, beat margarine, sugar and cinnamon with an electric mixer. Add eggs and beat until fluffy. Fold pineapple and bread cubes into the creamed mixture. Pour into the Crock- Pot. Cover and cook on Low for 6 to 7 hours or on High for 3 to 4 hours. Before serving top with chopped pecans and whipped topping if desired. Serve warm.

RICE PUDDING WITH PEARS

4	cups lite evaporated milk
3/4	cup sugar
1/2	cup short-grain rice, cooked
1	tablespoon cornstarch
2	eggs, beaten
1	can (16 ounces) pears, drained and chopped
1 1/2	teaspoons vanilla extract
1	tablespoon brown sugar
1/2	teaspoon ground cinnamon

Lightly grease Crock-Pot. In a mixing bowl, combine lite evaporated milk, sugar, and rice. Stir in the cornstarch. Gradually add the beaten egg. Fold in the pears and vanilla. Pour into Crock-Pot. Combine in a small bowl, the brown sugar and cinnamon. Sprinkle over the rice mixture. Cover and cook on High for 2 to 3 hours or until pudding is set. Serve.

TRIPLE CHOCOLATE SURPRISE

1	package chocolate cake mix
1	carton (8 ounces) sour cream
1	package instant chocolate pudding mix
1	cup chocolate chip morsels
3/4	cup oil
4	eggs
1	cup water

Spray Crock-Pot with non-stick cooking spray or lightly grease.

Mix cake mix, sour cream, pudding mix, chocolate chips, oil, eggs and water in bowl by hand. Pour into Crock-Pot. Cover and cook on Low 6 to 8 hours or on High for 3 to 4 hours. Serve hot or warm with ice cream or whipped cream topping.

PEACH COBBLER

¾	cup all-purpose baking mix, such as Bisquick
⅓	cup sugar
½	cup packed brown sugar
½	can evaporated milk
2	teaspoons margarine or butter, melted
2	eggs
3	large ripe peaches, mashed
2	teaspoons vanilla
¾	teaspoon cinnamon

Lightly grease Crock-Pot or spray with non-stick cooking spray.

In a large bowl, combine sugars and baking mix. Add eggs and vanilla. Stir. Pour in margarine and milk and stir. Mix in peaches and cinnamon, until well mixed. Pour into Crock-Pot. Cover and cook on Low for 6 to 8 hours or on High for 3 to 4 hours. Serve warm. Top with vanilla ice cream if desired.

CARROT CAKE

  2   eggs
  1   cup sugar
 ⅔   cup oil
 1½   cups flour
  1   teaspoon baking soda
 ½   teaspoon salt
  1   teaspoon cinnamon
 ¾   cup grated carrots
 ½   cup chopped nuts
  1   can (14 ounces) crushed pineapple in syrup,
       drained
  1   teaspoon vanilla

Beat together eggs, sugar and oil. Combine flour, soda, salt and cinnamon; add to sugar mixture and beat well. Stir in carrots, nuts, pineapple and vanilla.

Pour into greased and floured Bread 'n Cake Bake pan. Cover and place in Crock-Pot. Cover and bake on High for 2½ to 4 hours. *Serves 12 (3½- or 5-quart size).*

PEACH CRISP

 ⅔   cup old fashioned oats
 ⅓   cup all–purpose baking mix, such as
       Bisquick
 ½   teaspoon cinnamon
 ½   cup sugar
 ½   cup packed brown sugar
  4   cups sliced peaches

Lightly grease inside of Crock–Pot or spray with non–stick cooking spray.

Mix dry ingredients together in a large bowl. Stir in peaches until well blended. Pour into Crock–Pot. Cover and cook on Low 4 to 6 hours.

SOUR CREAM CHOCOLATE CHIP CAKE

$^1/_2$	cup margarine or butter
1	cup sugar
2	eggs
1	cup sour cream
1	teaspoon vanilla
$2^1/_2$	cups all-purpose flour
1	teaspoon baking soda
1	teaspoon baking powder
$^1/_2$	teaspoon salt
1	cup chocolate chips

Grease and flour inside of Bread N' Cake Bake Pan.

Cream margarine and sugar with an electric mixer. Add eggs and beat well. Mix in sour cream and vanilla.

In a small bowl, combine flour, baking soda, baking powder, and salt. Add to the creamed mixture. Stir in chocolate chips by hand. Pour into prepared Bread N' Cake Bake Pan. Place lid on pan. Place Bread N' Cake Bake Pan in Crock-Pot. Cover Crock-Pot and cook on High for 4 hours or until toothpick inserted comes out clean.

CHERRY PUDDING

This tasty cobbler bakes by the crust raising to the top and the cherry mixture sinks to the bottom of the Crock-Pot.

Mixture #1
- ³⁄₄   **cup sugar**
- 2   **tablespoons + 1¹⁄₂ teaspoons margarine or butter**
- ³⁄₄   **cup evaporated milk**
- 1¹⁄₂   **cups all-purpose flour**
- ³⁄₄   **teaspoon salt**
- 1¹⁄₂   **teaspoons baking powder**
- ¹⁄₈   **teaspoon cinnamon**

Mixture #2
- 2   **cans (16 ounces each) tart cherries and juice**
- 1   **teaspoon red food color**
- 2   **cups sugar**
- ¹⁄₄   **cup all-purpose flour**
- ¹⁄₄   **cup margarine or butter, melted**

Lightly grease inside of Crock-Pot.

Mixture #1: Combine sugar and margarine until crumbly. Add milk and other dry ingredients. Pour into Crock-Pot.

Mixture #2: Combine ingredients thoroughly until sugar is dissolved. Pour over Mixture #1 which will rise to the top during baking.

Cover and cook 3 to 4 hours on High or until dough is set and solid. Serve immediately. Top with vanilla ice cream if desired.

STRAWBERRY CHEESECAKE

Crust:
1¼ cups graham cracker crumbs
 ¼ cup margarine or butter, melted

Cheesecake:
  2 packages (8 ounces each) plus 1 (3-ounce) package cream cheese, softened
 ½ cup sugar
2-3 tablespoons flour
  3 eggs
 ½ cup strawberry preserves
  1 pint fresh strawberries

Preheat oven to 350°. Grease and flour inside of Bread N' Cake Bake Pan.

Mix together the graham cracker crumbs and melted margarine. Press into Bread N' Cake Bake Pan. Do not cover with the lid. Bake in oven for 5 to 7 minutes. Set aside.

With an electric mixer, cream the softened cream cheese until smooth; mix in sugar and flour. Add the eggs, or at a time; beat until fluffy. Fold in strawberry preserves. Pour over the baked crust in the Bread N' Cake Bake Pan. Place the lid on the pan. Place Bread N' Cake Bake Pan in Crock-Pot and cover. Cook on High 2½ to 3 hours. Remove when cheesecake is set. Remove pan from Crock-Pot. Allow to cool. Cover and refrigerate 8 hours. Remove and unmold onto plate, invert cheesecake onto serving platter. Top slices with fresh strawberries for serving.

BLACK FOREST CHEESECAKE

$^3/_4$ cup chocolate graham cracker cookies, crushed
3 packages (8 ounces each) fat-free cream cheese, softened
$1^1/_2$ cups sugar
$^3/_4$ cup egg substitute
1 cup semisweet chocolate morsels, melted
$^1/_4$ cup unsweetened cocoa
$1^1/_2$ teaspoons vanilla extract
1 carton (8 ounces) lite sour cream
1 can (21 ounces) cherry pie filling
$^3/_4$ cup reduced-calorie frozen whipped topping, thawed

Grease and flour Bread N' Cake Bake Pan. Spread crushed cookies in bottom of pan; set aside.

Beat cream cheese with an electric mixer until fluffy; gradually add sugar, beat well. Add egg substitute slowly, mixing well. Add melted chocolate, cocoa, and vanilla until well blended. Pour into prepared Bread N' Cake Bake Pan. Place lid on pan. Place in Crock-Pot. Cover Crock-Pot and cook on High for 4 hours. Remove from Crock-Pot and remove Bread N' Cake Bake Lid. Run a knife around edge of pan to release the sides. Let cool completely.

Place lid back on Bread N' Cake Bake Pan and refrigerate cheesecake for at least 8 hours. Remove cheesecake from refrigerator, invert pan and run bottom of Bread N' Cake Bake Pan briefly under warm water. On a plate turn invert Bread N' Cake Bake Pan and remove cheesecake. Then invert cheesecake right side up onto serving platter. Spread cheesecake with cherry pie filling. Spread with thawed frozen whipped topping or top each slice with a dollop of whipped topping. Slice and serve.

APPLESAUCE SPICE CAKE

- 1/4 **cup butter or margarine**
- 1/2 **cup sugar**
- 1 **egg**
- 1/2 **teaspoon vanilla**
- 3/4 **cup applesauce**
- 1 **cup flour**
- 1 **teaspoon baking soda**
- 1/4 **teaspoon cinnamon**
- 1/4 **teaspoon ground cloves**
- 1/4 **teaspoon nutmeg**
- 1/2 **cup raisins**
- 1/2 **cup chopped pecans**

Cream butter and sugar. Add egg and vanilla and beat well. Beat in applesauce. Combine flour, soda and spices and stir into creamed mixture. Blend in raisins and nuts.

Pour into greased and floured Bread 'n Cake Bake pan and cover. Place in Crock-Pot, cover and bake on High 2½ to 4 hours. *Serves 12.* Double recipe for 5-quart Crock-Pot.

TURTLE CHEESECAKE

Friends will not believe that this delicious cheesecake was prepared in the Crock-Pot

- 1 package (14 ounces) caramels
- ¾ cup evaporated milk
- 1¼ cups graham cracker crumbs
- ¼ cup margarine or butter, melted
- 1 cup chopped pecans
- 2 packages (8 ounces each) cream cheese, softened
- ½ cup sugar
- 2 eggs
- 1 teaspoon vanilla extract
- ¾ cup semisweet chocolate morsels, melted
  pecan halves

Preheat oven to 350°. Grease and flour inside of Bread N' Cake Bake Pan.

Combine crumbs and margarine, stirring well. Press crumb mixture evenly onto bottom of Bread N' Cake Bake Pan. Bake at 350° for 6 to 8 minutes Cool.

Unwrap caramels; combine caramels and milk in a heavy saucepan. Cook over low heat until melted, stirring often. Pour over Graham Cracker Crust. Sprinkle chopped pecans evenly over caramel layer, and set aside.

Beat cream cheese with an electric mixer until fluffy; gradually add sugar, mixing well. Add eggs, one at a time, beating after each addition. Stir in vanilla and chocolate until well blended. Spoon over pecan layer in Bread N' Cake Bake Pan. Cover with lid and place in Crock-Pot. Cover Crock-Pot and bake 3 hours on High or until set. Remove from Crock-Pot, run a knife around edge of cheesecake and allow to cool.

Cover and chill at least 8 hours. Remove cheesecake from Bread N' Cake Bake Pan. Place cheesecake onto serving plate with graham cracker crust on the bottom. Arrange pecan halves around top edge of cheesecake. Cut and serve.

HOT FUDGE CAKE

1	cup packed brown sugar
1	cup all-purpose flour
1/4	cup plus 3 tablespoons unsweetened cocoa
3/4	cup packed brown sugar
2	teaspoons baking powder
1/2	teaspoon salt
1/2	cup milk
2	tablespoons margarine or butter, melted
1/2	teaspoon vanilla
1 3/4	cups boiling water

Mix 1 cup brown sugar, the flour, 3 tablespoons cocoa, baking powder, and salt together in a mixing bowl. Stir in the milk, margarine, and vanilla. Spread over the bottom of the Crock-Pot.

In another bowl, mix together the 3/4 cup brown sugar and 1/4 cup cocoa. Sprinkle evenly over mixture in the Crock-Pot. Do not stir.

Then pour in the boiling water. Do not stir. Cover and cook on High 2 to 3 hours until a toothpick inserted comes out clean. Serve warm with ice cream or whipped topping if desired.

(recipe for 3 1/2-quart)

TRIPLE LAYER CHEESECAKE GLAZED WITH CHOCOLATE

Chocolate lover's delight in this triple layer cheesecake.

- 2 cups crushed chocolate wafer cookies
- ¾ cup sugar, divided
- ¼ cup plus 1 tablespoon margarine or butter, melted
- 2 packages (8 ounces each) cream cheese, softened and divided
- 3 eggs
- 1 teaspoon vanilla extract, divided
- 2 squares (1 ounce each) semi–sweet chocolate, melted
- 1 ⅓ cups sour cream, divided
- ⅓ cup firmly packed dark brown sugar
- 1 tablespoon all–purpose flour
- ¼ cup chopped pecans
- 5 ounces cream cheese, softened
- ¼ teaspoon almond extract

Chocolate Glaze:

- 6 squares (1 ounce each) semi–sweet chocolate
- ¼ cup margarine or butter
- ¾ cup powdered sugar
- 2 tablespoons water
- 1 teaspoon vanilla extract

Grease and flour inside of Bread N' Cake Bake Pan.

Combine cookie crumbs, ¼ cup sugar, and margarine in a small bowl. Press into bottom of Bread N' Cake Bake Pan. Set aside.

Combine 1 8-ounce package cream cheese and ¼ cup sugar in a mixing bowl and beat well with an electric mixer. Add 1 egg and ¼ teaspoon vanilla; beat well. Stir in melted chocolate and ⅓ cup sour cream. Spoon over the chocolate crust.

Combine in a small bowl the remaining 8-ounce package of cream cheese, brown sugar, and flour; beat well. Add 1 egg and ½ teaspoon vanilla; beat well. Fold in the pecans. Spoon this mixture over the chocolate layer. Do not stir.

In a small mixing bowl, combine the 5 ounces of cream cheese and ¼ cup sugar; beat well. Add 1 egg; beat well. Stir in 1 cup of sour cream, ¼ teaspoon vanilla, and almond extract. Spoon over the pecan layer. Do not stir. Cover Bread N' Cake Bake Pan with lid.

Place pan in Crock–Pot. Cover Crock–Pot and bake on High for 4 hours or until set. Remove Bread N' Cake Bake Pan from Crock–Pot. Remove the lid from pan. Allow cheesecake to cool completely. Refrigerate at least 8 hours. To serve, unmold cheesecake from Bread N' Cake Bake Pan onto plate and then invert onto another plate. Prepare glaze as directed and spread over cheesecake. Cut into slices and serve.

CHOCOLATE NUT CAKE

The secret in this recipe is the mashed potatoes which makes the cake deliciously rich and moist.

- 2/3 **cup margarine or butter**
- 1 1/2 **cups sugar**
- 4 **eggs**
- 1 **cup prepared instant mashed potatoes**
- 2 **cups all-purpose flour**
- 2/3 **cup unsweetened cocoa**
- 2 **teaspoons powder**
- 1 **teaspoon salt**
- 1/2 **teaspoon cinnamon**
- 1/2 **cup milk**
- 1/2 **cup chopped pecans**

Grease and flour inside of Bread N' Cake Bake Pan.

Cream margarine with an electric mixer. Beat in sugar and eggs until smooth. Mix in cooled potatoes.

In a small bowl, combine flour, cocoa, baking powder, salt, and cinnamon. Add to the creamed mixture alternately with the milk. Fold in nuts. Pour into a prepared Bread N' Cake Bake Pan. Place lid on Pan. Set Bread N' Cake Bake Pan inside Crock-Pot. Cover Crock-Pot and cook on High for 3 to 4 hours or until toothpick inserted comes out clean. Check for doneness after 3 hours. When cake is done remove pan from Crock-Pot and let cool for 5 to 10 minutes. Invert cake onto plate and then invert again onto serving platter. Serve.

STEWED FRUIT AND DUMPLINGS

For this recipe simply use your favorite fruit, for a tasty dessert with a dumpling crust.

2	pints fresh or frozen fruit, such as straw-berries, raspberries, blueberries, peaches, etc.
1/2	cups plus 2 tablespoons sugar
1/2	cup warm water
2	tablespoons quick–cooking tapioca
2	cups all–purpose flour
2 1/2	teaspoons baking powder
1/2	teaspoon salt
5	tablespoons margarine or butter, cut in cubes
1/2	cup milk
1	egg
2	tablespoons brown sugar

In the Crock–Pot, combine the fruit, the 1/2 cup sugar, the water, and tapioca. Cover and cook on Low for 5 to 6 hours or on High for 2 1/2 to 3 hours or until the fruit has formed a thick sauce.

In a mixing bowl, combine the flour, the 2 tablespoons sugar, baking powder, and salt. Use a pastry blender or 2 knives to cut in the margarine until the mixture resembles coarse meal. In a small bowl, stir together the milk and the egg. Pour the milk and egg mixture into the flour mixture and stir until a soft dough is formed.

Turn the Crock–Pot to High if it is on Low. Drop the dough by teaspoonfuls on top of the fruit. Cover and cook 30 minutes to 1 hour, until a toothpick inserted into the dumplings comes out clean. Sprinkle with brown sugar. Serve warm.

SWEET POTATOES AND PINEAPPLE PUDDING

3   pounds sweet potatoes, peeled and shredded
2   cans (8 ounces) crushed pineapple in unsweetened juice, undrained
1   can (12 ounces) evaporated milk
1¼ cups brown sugar, firmly packed
6   tablespoons margarine or butter, cut in cubes
3   eggs, slightly beaten
1   teaspoon ground cinnamon
1/2 teaspoon nutmeg

Lightly grease Crock-Pot. In Crock-Pot, combine sweet potatoes, pineapple, evaporated milk, brown sugar, margarine, eggs, cinnamon, and nutmeg. Cover and cook on Low 7 to 8 hours or on High 4 hours, stirring every 2 hours until the potatoes are tender. Serve hot or at room temperature.

Note: This dish may appear to be curdling, however it will come together toward the end of cooking. *Serves 10 to 12.*

HINTS

TO BROWN OR NOT TO BROWN?

When meat is prepared in the Crock-Pot Slow Cooker it does not brown as it would in a skillet or oven. It is not necessary to brown meat before slow cooking, however, the meat should be wiped thoroughly to absorb all excess juices and package residue. Browning meat before cooking in the Crock-Pot helps eliminate fats, as too much fat can cause overcooking. Also, if you prefer the flavor of browned meat or vegetables, heat a small amount of oil in a skillet; add meat or vegetables and brown on medium-high heat. Turn meat or vegetables over and brown other side. Add to Crock-Pot Slow Cooker and follow our directions for the recipe.

A WAY WITH VEGETABLES

Vegetables tend to cook slowly; cut them into $1/8$- $1/4$-inch slices and place them near the bottom of the Crock-Pot.

CROCK-POT CRISPING

Use your Crock-Pot to revive stale potato chips and crackers. Place them in the pot, but do not cover. Heat on Low setting for 2 to 4 hours. Voila! They're crisp and warm.

REMOVABLE STONEWARE

Foods may be prepared the night before and refrigerated in the stoneware bowl. A few hints to remember:

- Place stoneware bowl in heating base and turn on to desired setting. Bowl and food do not need to be allowed to come to room temperature. Use maximum cooking time.

- Do not preheat electrical base.

- If preparing dishes with rice or pasta, do not add liquid until just before cooking.

- Potatoes may be kept from darkening by rinsing in a solution of 1 cup water and $1/2$ teaspoon cream of tartar. Drain and proceed as recipe directs, keeping the heat on.

   Your Crock-Pot makes an ideal server for a hot punch or hot dip. Keep it on Low setting to maintain the proper serving temperature (creamy dips, however, should not be left uncovered for more than 2 hours).

FOR CAREFREE CASSEROLES

Slow cooking is ideal for casseroles. It gives the different ingredients plenty of time to cook together, creating a mellower blend of flavors. Best of all, casseroles can be put together the night before and refrigerated in a bowl. The following morning, pour the contents into a a lightly greased Crock-Pot. Cover and cook the recommended time. On models with a removable stoneware bowl, fill and refrigerate stoneware bowl.

HERBS AND SPICES: THE FLAVOR SAVORS

It's best to use whole herbs and spices rather than the crushed or ground forms. The flavor of crushed or ground herbs and spices tends to dissipate during the extended cooking times called for in the Crock-Pot. Moreover, the leaf form takes a much longer time to release its flavor; hence it will be at its peak at serving time. Always taste before serving and adjust the seasonings if necessary.

REMOVAL OF EXCESS FAT

• Take time to trim and remove excess fat from meat before cooking to reduce the amount of fat that accumulates during cooking.

• When serving a stew or soup, skim off excess fat with a slice of bread, use a spoon, or use a straining device designed to remove fat from liquids before spooning into dishes.

A WAY WITH BREADS AND CAKES

• Do not over-beat breads and cakes. Follow recommended mixing times, usually 2 minutes.

• Never place baking pan on meat rack.

• Do not add water to Crock-Pot unless it is specifically requested in the recipe.

• After baking breads or cakes, allow to cool 5 minutes, then invert pan on cooling rack or plate.

• To reheat breads, cakes or puddings, wrap securely in aluminum foil and place in Crock-Pot. Cover and heat on High setting for 1 to 1½ hours (on Low setting for 2 to 3 hours).

CROCK-POT BAKING TIPS

- You will note that many of these bread and cake recipes call for the use of the accessory Bread 'N Cake Bake pan. Write to The Rival Company for ordering information.

- To achieve the best volume in baked goods, always use large fresh eggs.

- The dough for Crock-Pot yeast breads has a different consistency than you might expect. In fact, it's more like a batter than a dough— and that's as it should be.

ADAPTING RECIPES TO THE CROCK-POT

Recipes that lend themselves to Crock-Pot cooking are limitless. Almost any recipe requiring baking or simmering will work beautifully. Here are a few simple guidelines that will help you prepare your favorites in the Crock-Pot:

- Allow sufficient time on "Low"setting.

- Remember — liquids don't "boil away" as in conventional cooking. Usually you'll have more liquid at the end of cooking instead of less. Try reducing the amount of liquid in the recipe by about one-half. The exception would be soup recipes or recipes with long grain converted rice which will need the same amount of liquid or ¼ cup liquid per ¼ cup raw rice.

- Many preparatory steps are not necessary. Vegetables do not need to be browned or sauteed. In most cases, all ingredients can be added to the Crock-Pot in the beginning and allowed to cook all day. Exception: milk, sour cream, or cream should be added during the last hour of cooking.

- Crock-Pot Slow Cooker cooks so gently that a few extra hours on Low need not worry you. Any recipe may be cooked on High for the first two hours to reduce cooking time, then turn to Low.

If recipe says:	Cook in Crock-Pot:
15 to 30 minutes	1½ to 2½ hours on High or 4 to 8 hours on Low*

| 35 to 40 minutes | 3 to 4 hours on High or 6 to 10 hours on Low |
| 50 min to 3 hours | 4 to 6 hours on High or 8 to 18 hours on Low |

* Most uncooked meat and vegetable combinations will require at least 8 hours on Low.

SUBSTITUTE TO SUIT

You can tailor any main-dish recipe to suit your own taste preferences. It's easy. Simply, substitute liquids, condensed soups, seasonings, or vegetables of your own choosing for the ones suggested in the recipes — providing, of course, the amounts are the same. Here are a few examples:

• Substitute beef or chicken broth for wine or sherry.

• Try cream of chicken soup instead of cream of celery.

• Hate tomatoes? Replace a 16-ounce can of tomatoes with 1 can of condensed cream soup plus 6 ounces water.

• Use sliced celery instead of onions or green pepper.

• Omit the seasonings — or add just before serving.

MAKING FOIL HANDLES

Foil handles make it easier to lift Mexican tortilla stack meals or meat loaves out of the Crock-Pot. To make the handles, tear off three 20 x 3-inch strips of heavy foil or use regular foil folded to double thickness. Crisscross the foil strips in a spoke design.

If preparing a Mexican tortilla stack meal, place the foil strips in a spoke design in the Crock-Pot. Then layer the tortillas and meat and cheese mixtures on top of the foil in the Crock-Pot.

If preparing a meat loaf, place the foil handles on a large sheet of waxed paper. Shape the meat loaf on the spoke design. Lift the ends of the handles to transfer the loaf to the Crock-Pot.

When ready to serve, simply lift the foil handles from the Crock-Pot and remove the meal to a serving dish.

CROCK-POT SAFETY

Crock-Pots generally have short supply cords to reduce the hazards resulting from entanglement of tripping over a longer cord. An extension cord may be used, however, **the marked electrical rating shall be at least as great as the electrical rating of this appliance.** The extension cord should not be allowed to drape over the tabletop where it can be pulled on by children or tripped over.

If the stoneware has been preheated or is hot to the touch, do not pour in cold foods. Do not preheat Crock-Pot before using unless specified in recipe. The Crock-Pot should be at room temperature before adding hot foods.

Do not reheat foods in the Crock-Pot.

A NOTE ABOUT PORK

Because fat can cause your dish to overcook and lose flavor, be sure your pork choice is well trimmed. Pre-brown ribs, roasts and other fatty cuts by broiling for 20 minutes; drain well. If using chops, choose 1-inch thick loin chops (rib chops are too fat and too small to cook satisfactorily).

A WAY WITH CHICKEN

Be sure to wash chicken well and pat dry — especially if you don't plan to pre-brown it. You might even try soaking it in lightly salted water in the refrigerator for 8 to 10 hours before using it in the Crock-Pot — some say the flavor is even better. If you like your chicken firm and dry, reduce the amount of liquid called for in the recipe.

KNOW YOUR BEANS

One type of dried beans may substitute for any other type providing the measure is the same. Tailor the bean soup recipes in this book to suit your own tastes.